Conquering Fear: Empowering V-

Speak with Cor.

Oscar Orlov

Copyright © [2023]

Author: Oscar Orlov

Title: Conquering Fear: Empowering Yourself to Speak with Confidence

This book is a self-published work by the author Oscar Orlov

ISBN:

TABLE OF CONTENTS

Chapter 3: Developing Effective Communication Skills   20

Chapter 4: Practicing and Preparing for Public Speaking 38

Chapter 1: Understanding Fear and Its Impact on Communication

The Nature of Fear

Fear is a powerful emotion that has the potential to hold us back from reaching our true potential. It is a natural response to perceived threats or danger, but it can also be paralyzing and prevent us from taking necessary risks and seizing opportunities. In this subchapter, we will explore the nature of fear and how understanding it can empower us to speak with confidence.

Fear is deeply rooted in our evolutionary history. It served as a survival mechanism, helping our ancestors avoid dangerous situations and predators. However, in the modern world, fear often manifests in response to non-life-threatening situations, such as public speaking. This fear is often irrational, but that does not make it any less real or intense.

Understanding the nature of fear is the first step towards conquering it. Fear is often fueled by negative thoughts and beliefs. We might worry about being judged, making mistakes, or embarrassing ourselves in front of others. These thoughts create a cycle of fear that can be difficult to break.

It is important to recognize that fear is not a reflection of our abilities or worth. It is a normal human emotion that everyone experiences to some degree. By acknowledging and accepting our fears, we can begin to take steps towards overcoming them.

One effective strategy for conquering fear is through gradual exposure. This involves gradually exposing ourselves to the situations that trigger our fear, starting with small steps and gradually increasing the intensity. For example, if public speaking is a fear, we can start by speaking in front of a small group of trusted friends and gradually work our way up to larger audiences.

Another powerful tool for conquering fear is reframing our mindset. Instead of viewing fear as a threat, we can choose to see it as an opportunity for growth and learning. By embracing fear and stepping out of our comfort zones, we can expand our horizons and develop new skills.

Ultimately, conquering fear requires practice and perseverance. It is not a one-time event, but rather an ongoing journey. By understanding the nature of fear and taking proactive steps to overcome it, we can empower ourselves to speak with confidence and unlock our full potential.

Remember, fear is a natural part of the human experience. It does not define us, but rather presents an opportunity for growth and self-discovery. Embrace your fears, challenge yourself, and watch as your confidence soars.

The Link between Fear and Communication

Fear, an innate human emotion, can often hinder our ability to communicate effectively. In the realm of public speaking, fear can be particularly crippling, preventing individuals from expressing themselves with confidence and clarity. Understanding the link between fear and communication is essential for anyone looking to overcome their anxieties and become a powerful speaker.

When we experience fear, our bodies enter a state of fight or flight, triggered by the release of stress hormones such as adrenaline. This physiological response can have a profound impact on our ability to communicate. In moments of fear, our heart rate increases, our breathing becomes shallow, and our muscles tense up. These physical manifestations can make it challenging to speak coherently, leading to stammering, stuttering, or even complete silence.

Fear also affects our mental state, causing us to lose focus and become overwhelmed with self-doubt. Negative thoughts and beliefs about our abilities can creep in, further exacerbating our communication difficulties. We may worry about being judged or ridiculed, leading to a fear of public humiliation. These fears can create a vicious cycle, as our anxiety increases with each negative experience, making future speeches even more daunting.

To conquer fear and improve our communication skills, it is crucial to develop strategies that address both the physical and mental aspects of fear. Deep breathing exercises, for instance, can help regulate our heart rate and induce a sense of calmness. By consciously taking slow, deep breaths, we can counteract the physical symptoms of fear and regain control over our bodies.

Another effective technique is positive visualization. By visualizing successful speeches and positive outcomes, we can reprogram our minds to focus on success rather than failure. Affirmations and self-talk can also be powerful tools in combating fear. Replacing negative thoughts with positive ones can help boost our confidence and shift our mindset towards a more optimistic outlook.

Additionally, seeking support from others can be invaluable in overcoming fear. Joining public speaking groups or seeking the guidance of a speaking coach can provide a safe and supportive environment for practicing and refining our communication skills. Surrounding ourselves with individuals who understand our fears and can provide constructive feedback can greatly improve our confidence and ability to speak with conviction.

In conclusion, fear and communication are intrinsically linked. Understanding the impact of fear on our bodies and minds is vital for anyone seeking to conquer their anxieties and become a confident speaker. By implementing strategies that address the physical and mental aspects of fear, and by seeking support from others, we can empower ourselves to overcome our fears and communicate with confidence. Remember, everyone is capable of speaking fearlessly; it is merely a matter of unlocking our true potential.

Identifying Fear in Communication Situations

Fear is a powerful emotion that can have a significant impact on our ability to communicate effectively. Whether you are giving a speech, engaging in a conversation, or participating in a group discussion, it is crucial to recognize and address your fears to ensure you can speak with confidence. In this subchapter, we will explore the different ways fear manifests itself in communication situations and provide strategies to conquer these fears.

One common fear in communication is the fear of public speaking. Many people experience anxiety when standing in front of an audience, fearing judgment, embarrassment, or forgetting what to say. It is important to recognize the physical symptoms of fear, such as a racing heart, sweaty palms, or trembling voice, as these can be indicators of underlying fear. By acknowledging these signs, you can start to address the root cause of your fear and work towards overcoming it.

Another fear that often arises in communication situations is the fear of rejection or criticism. This fear may cause individuals to hesitate in expressing their thoughts or ideas, fearing that others may disagree or judge them harshly. By identifying this fear, you can develop strategies to build your self-confidence and learn to embrace constructive feedback, recognizing that it is an opportunity for growth rather than a personal attack.

Furthermore, fear can also arise from a lack of knowledge or preparation. The fear of not knowing enough or being unprepared for a communication situation can be paralyzing. However, by identifying this fear, you can take proactive steps to increase your knowledge and level of preparedness, such as conducting thorough research or practicing your speech or presentation multiple times.

To conquer fear in communication situations, it is essential to develop self-awareness and identify the specific fears that hinder your ability to speak with confidence. By recognizing the signs of fear, whether they are physical, emotional, or mental, you can begin to address and manage them effectively. Additionally, seeking support from peers, mentors, or professionals in public speaking can provide valuable guidance and encouragement throughout your journey.

Remember, fear is a natural response, but it should not limit your potential to communicate effectively. By identifying fear in communication situations and employing strategies to conquer it, you can empower yourself to speak with confidence and convey your message with impact.

Chapter 2: Overcoming Internal Barriers

Recognizing Self-Doubt and Negative Self-Talk

Self-doubt and negative self-talk are two common obstacles that can hinder your ability to conquer fear and speak with confidence. These internal struggles often arise when we face challenging situations or prepare to deliver a speech on fear. Understanding and recognizing these negative patterns is the first step towards overcoming them.

Self-doubt is the voice inside our heads that tells us we are not good enough or capable of achieving our goals. It can stem from past failures, criticism, or a lack of self-confidence. When preparing to speak on fear, self-doubt can manifest as thoughts like, "I'm going to mess up," or "Nobody will listen to me." These thoughts can be paralyzing and prevent us from taking action.

Negative self-talk is the inner dialogue that focuses on our weaknesses rather than our strengths. It often involves harsh and critical statements that undermine our self-esteem. For instance, when preparing to speak on fear, negative self-talk may sound like, "I always stumble over my words," or "I'm not as good as other speakers." This negative internal dialogue can erode our confidence and make it challenging to deliver an impactful speech.

To recognize self-doubt and negative self-talk, it is crucial to develop self-awareness. Start paying attention to your thoughts and the language you use when preparing for a speech on fear. Notice any patterns of self-doubt or negative self-talk that arise. By becoming aware of these patterns, you can consciously challenge and reframe them.

One effective technique is to replace negative thoughts with positive affirmations. For example, if you catch yourself thinking, "I'm going to mess up," replace it with, "I am well-prepared and capable of delivering a powerful speech." By consciously choosing positive affirmations, you can rewire your brain to focus on your strengths and build self-confidence.

Another helpful strategy is to seek support from others. Share your fears and concerns with a trusted friend, mentor, or support group. Often, talking about our insecurities can provide a fresh perspective and reassurance that we are not alone. Additionally, receiving constructive feedback and encouragement from others can help counteract self-doubt and negative self-talk.

Recognizing self-doubt and negative self-talk is an essential step towards empowering yourself to speak with confidence. By developing self-awareness, challenging negative thoughts, and seeking support, you can overcome these obstacles and deliver a compelling speech on fear. Remember, it is normal to experience self-doubt, but it doesn't define your capabilities. With practice and perseverance, you can conquer fear and become a confident speaker.

Building Self-Confidence through Positive Affirmations

In the journey of conquering fear and empowering yourself to speak with confidence, building self-confidence is a crucial step. One effective tool that can aid in this process is the practice of positive affirmations. Positive affirmations are powerful statements that can help reprogram your mind and replace negative thoughts with positive ones. By incorporating positive affirmations into your daily routine, you can train your mind to believe in your abilities and develop a strong sense of self-confidence.

Positive affirmations work by challenging and reversing negative self-talk. We often harbor self-doubt and fear of failure, which can hinder our ability to speak confidently in public. However, by consciously integrating positive affirmations into our lives, we can counteract these limiting beliefs. For example, repeating statements like "I am confident and capable of speaking in public" or "I believe in myself and my ability to deliver a powerful speech" can gradually shift your mindset and boost your self-confidence.

The key to effective positive affirmations lies in their repetition and consistency. It is crucial to make positive affirmations a part of your daily routine, reinforcing them until they become ingrained in your subconscious mind. Repetition helps to reinforce positive beliefs, allowing them to replace any lingering self-doubt.

To maximize the impact of positive affirmations, it is essential to engage both your mind and body. While repeating affirmations, focus on your breathing, visualize yourself speaking with confidence, and feel the emotions associated with success. This holistic approach enhances the effectiveness of positive affirmations, making them more powerful in building self-confidence.

Moreover, it is important to remember that positive affirmations are not a magic solution. They are a tool that, when combined with consistent effort and practice, can significantly contribute to overcoming fear and building self-confidence. Alongside affirmations, it is essential to actively seek opportunities to practice public speaking, take courses, and learn from experienced speakers. This combination of inner work and practical experience will help you develop the necessary skills and self-assurance to speak confidently in any situation.

In conclusion, positive affirmations are a valuable tool for building self-confidence and conquering the fear of public speaking. By incorporating positive affirmations into your daily routine, challenging negative self-talk, and reinforcing positive beliefs, you can gradually transform your mindset and develop unwavering self-confidence. Remember that building self-confidence is a journey, and positive affirmations serve as a powerful ally in this process.

Challenging Limiting Beliefs about Speaking

In our journey to conquer fear and empower ourselves to speak with confidence, we must address the limiting beliefs that hold us back. These beliefs are like invisible chains that restrict our potential and prevent us from fully expressing ourselves. However, by challenging these beliefs, we can break free and discover a newfound sense of confidence in our speech.

One of the most common limiting beliefs about speaking is the fear of judgment and criticism. Many of us worry about what others will think of our words, fearing that we will be laughed at or ridiculed. This fear can be paralyzing, preventing us from speaking up and sharing our thoughts and ideas. However, it's important to remember that everyone has the right to their own opinion, and not everyone will agree with us. By embracing this reality and focusing on the value of our own voice, we can overcome this limiting belief and speak with authenticity and conviction.

Another limiting belief is the idea that we are not knowledgeable or experienced enough to speak on a certain topic. We may believe that we need to be an expert in order to have something valuable to say. However, it's important to recognize that everyone has unique perspectives and insights to offer. Our personal stories and experiences hold immense power and can resonate with others in ways that expertise alone cannot. By letting go of the need for perfection and embracing our own unique voice, we can challenge this belief and speak with confidence about our fears and the ways in which we have overcome them.

Lastly, many of us believe that we must always have something profound or groundbreaking to say in order to speak up. This belief can lead to self-doubt and silence, as we feel that our words are not worthy unless they are revolutionary. However, it's crucial to remember that simple truths and genuine emotions can have a profound impact on others. By embracing our vulnerability and sharing our authentic selves, we can challenge this belief and find the power in our own voice.

In conclusion, challenging the limiting beliefs about speaking is essential for conquering fear and empowering ourselves to speak with confidence. By addressing the fear of judgment, letting go of the need for expertise, and embracing our own authenticity, we can break free from the chains that hold us back and discover the transformative power of our own words. Remember, your voice matters, and by challenging your limiting beliefs, you can unleash your true potential in the realm of speech on fear.

Chapter 3: Developing Effective Communication Skills

Enhancing Verbal Communication

Verbal communication plays a pivotal role in our lives, affecting how we express ourselves, connect with others, and conquer our fears. Whether it's delivering a speech on fear or engaging in everyday conversations, mastering the art of effective verbal communication is essential for personal growth and empowerment. In this subchapter, we will explore various techniques and strategies to enhance your verbal communication skills, allowing you to speak with confidence and overcome the fear that often accompanies public speaking.

First and foremost, improving your verbal communication begins with developing a strong foundation of self-awareness. Understanding your strengths and weaknesses as a speaker will enable you to identify areas for improvement. Take time to reflect on your speaking style, tone, and body language. Are you speaking too fast or too softly? Do you maintain eye contact with your audience? By recognizing these aspects, you can actively work on refining your delivery and making necessary adjustments.

Another crucial aspect of enhancing verbal communication is effective storytelling. Storytelling is a powerful tool that captivates listeners and helps them connect with your message. Incorporate personal anecdotes and relatable experiences to engage your audience and evoke emotions. By crafting compelling narratives, you can effectively convey your ideas and overcome fear by connecting on a deeper level with your listeners.

Additionally, practice and preparation are essential elements in improving verbal communication. The more you practice, the more comfortable and confident you become. Utilize techniques such as role-playing or recording yourself to gain valuable feedback. This will allow you to identify areas that need improvement and refine your delivery. Prepare yourself mentally by visualizing success and positive outcomes before any speaking engagement. This visualization technique helps alleviate fear and boosts your confidence.

Furthermore, active listening is a fundamental aspect of effective verbal communication. Paying attention to your audience's reactions and feedback allows you to gauge their level of engagement and make necessary adjustments. Engage in active dialogue by asking questions, encouraging participation, and giving room for others to express their thoughts. This not only enhances your communication skills but also helps build rapport and trust with your listeners.

In conclusion, enhancing verbal communication is a transformative journey that empowers individuals to conquer their fears and speak with confidence. By developing self-awareness, incorporating storytelling, practicing diligently, and actively listening, you can elevate your communication skills to the next level. Whether you are delivering a speech on fear or engaging in everyday conversations, these techniques will enable you to connect with your audience authentically and effectively. Embrace this journey of growth, and witness how your enhanced verbal communication skills empower you to conquer fear and speak with unwavering confidence.

Speaking Clearly and Articulately

One of the most crucial aspects of conquering fear and speaking with confidence is learning to speak clearly and articulately. Whether you are delivering a speech on fear or any other topic, the way you communicate your ideas can greatly influence how your audience perceives you and the message you are trying to convey. In this subchapter, we will explore various techniques and strategies to help you improve your speaking skills and leave a lasting impact on your audience.

First and foremost, it is essential to work on your pronunciation and enunciation. Clear pronunciation ensures that your words are easily understood by your listeners, while proper enunciation helps you articulate each syllable with precision and clarity. Practice speaking slowly and deliberately, paying attention to the correct placement of your tongue, lips, and teeth for each sound. Regularly engaging in exercises that focus on specific speech sounds can significantly enhance your ability to articulate words effectively.

Another important aspect of speaking clearly and articulately is maintaining a good pace and rhythm. Speaking too fast can make it difficult for your audience to follow your thoughts, while speaking too slow can cause them to lose interest. Find a balance that allows you to speak at a comfortable pace, pausing appropriately to emphasize key points or give your listeners time to process the information you are sharing.

In addition to pronunciation and pace, incorporating vocal variety into your delivery is crucial. Using variations in pitch, volume, and tone can help you capture your audience's attention and create a more engaging experience. Experiment with different vocal techniques, such as emphasizing certain words or phrases, using inflection to convey various emotions, and modulating your voice to match the content of your speech.

Lastly, remember to be mindful of your body language and non-verbal cues while speaking. Maintaining eye contact with your audience, using appropriate hand gestures, and standing or sitting with good posture can enhance your overall delivery. Your body language should be confident and open, reflecting your self-assurance and passion for the topic you are presenting.

By honing your skills in speaking clearly and articulately, you will be able to effectively communicate your ideas, conquer your fear, and leave a lasting impact on your audience. Practice regularly, seek feedback from trusted individuals, and embrace every speaking opportunity as a chance to grow and improve. Remember, the more you invest in developing your speaking skills, the more empowered and confident you will become in conquering fear and delivering impactful speeches.

Using Effective Body Language

When it comes to conquering fear and empowering yourself to speak with confidence, mastering the art of effective body language is essential. Our body language communicates more than we may realize, and by understanding and utilizing it effectively, we can enhance our speeches on fear and captivate our audience.

First and foremost, it is crucial to maintain good posture. Standing tall with your shoulders back not only exudes confidence but also allows for better breath control and voice projection. By demonstrating an upright posture, you convey a sense of authority and credibility, immediately capturing the attention of your audience.

In addition to posture, gestures play a vital role in effective body language. Using purposeful and controlled gestures can help emphasize key points and keep your audience engaged. However, be sure to avoid excessive or distracting movements that may take away from your message. Remember, your gestures should be natural and complementary to your speech.

Eye contact is another powerful tool in conveying confidence and connecting with your audience. Maintaining eye contact demonstrates sincerity and builds trust. By scanning the room and making eye contact with different individuals, you create a sense of inclusivity and make your speech more personal and relatable. However, be mindful not to stare or avoid eye contact altogether, as this may make your audience feel uncomfortable.

Facial expressions are another essential aspect of effective body language. Your face should reflect the emotions and sentiments you wish to convey. A genuine smile, for example, can instantly create a positive atmosphere and help alleviate tension. Likewise, using appropriate expressions to match the tone of your speech can enhance your message and make it more impactful.

Finally, paying attention to your overall body movements and positioning can greatly enhance your speech on fear. Avoid crossing your arms, as this can create a barrier between you and your audience, making it harder to connect. Instead, keep your arms open and use them to support your words. Be mindful of your stance and avoid fidgeting, as it can indicate nervousness and distract from your message.

In conclusion, effective body language is a powerful tool for conquering fear and empowering yourself to speak with confidence. By mastering good posture, purposeful gestures, maintaining eye contact, displaying appropriate facial expressions, and being mindful of your overall body movements, you can create a strong and captivating presence during your speech on fear. Remember, your body language should align with your message and help convey your thoughts and emotions effectively to your audience. With practice and awareness, you can utilize body language to its fullest potential and become a confident and impactful speaker.

Active Listening and Responding

In the pursuit of conquering fear and empowering oneself to speak with confidence, it is essential to develop the skills of active listening and responding. These skills play a crucial role in effective communication, especially when delivering speeches on fear. Whether you are addressing a small group or a large audience, active listening and responding can greatly enhance your ability to connect with your listeners and convey your message with clarity and conviction.

Active listening involves more than just hearing the words being spoken. It requires giving your full attention to the speaker, both verbally and non-verbally. By maintaining eye contact, nodding, and providing verbal cues such as "I understand" or "Go on," you show the speaker that you are actively engaged and interested in what they have to say. This not only encourages the speaker to open up and share more but also helps you gain a deeper understanding of their perspective on fear.

Furthermore, active listening allows you to pick up on non-verbal cues, such as body language and tone of voice, which can provide valuable insights into the speaker's emotions and intentions. This information can help you tailor your response accordingly, ensuring that your message is delivered in a way that resonates with your audience.

In addition to active listening, effective responding is crucial when delivering speeches on fear. Responding involves providing thoughtful and well-crafted feedback or commentary to the speaker's ideas or concerns. This can be done through verbal responses, such as asking clarifying questions or providing relevant examples, as well as non-verbal responses, such as nodding or smiling to show support and encouragement.

By responding actively, you not only validate the speaker's thoughts and feelings but also create a safe and inclusive environment for open dialogue. This is particularly important when discussing sensitive topics like fear, as it allows individuals to share their experiences and learn from one another.

In conclusion, mastering the art of active listening and responding is vital for anyone seeking to conquer fear and speak with confidence. By actively engaging with speakers and responding thoughtfully, you can foster meaningful connections, gain a deeper understanding of fear, and effectively convey your message to your audience. So, the next time you find yourself delivering a speech on fear, remember to listen attentively and respond with empathy and insight.

Mastering Non-Verbal Communication

In the world of public speaking, words are only a part of the equation. Non-verbal communication, including body language and facial expressions, plays a crucial role in conveying your message effectively and connecting with your audience. To truly conquer fear and empower yourself to speak with confidence, mastering non-verbal communication is essential.

Body language is a powerful tool that can either enhance or undermine your speech on fear. By becoming aware of your body movements, you can project confidence and engage your audience. Start by maintaining an open posture, standing tall with your shoulders back. This simple adjustment exudes self-assurance and helps to calm your nerves.

Gestures also play a vital role in non-verbal communication. Appropriate hand movements can emphasize key points and add visual interest to your speech. Avoid excessive or repetitive gestures, as they can be distracting. Instead, aim for natural and purposeful movements that complement your words.

Maintaining eye contact is another crucial aspect of non-verbal communication. By making eye contact with individuals in your audience, you establish a connection and convey sincerity. Engaging with your listeners on a personal level helps to build trust and credibility. However, be sure to scan the room and maintain eye contact with various individuals, as focusing on only one person can make others feel left out.

Facial expressions are the window to your emotions and thoughts. Expressiveness is key when delivering a speech on fear. Use your face to convey your passion, conviction, and empathy. A genuine smile can instantly put your audience at ease and make them more receptive to your message. Practice in front of a mirror or record yourself to become more aware of your facial expressions and make necessary adjustments.

Non-verbal communication also extends to voice modulation and pace. Varying your tone, volume, and speed can add depth and interest to your speech. Pausing strategically allows your audience to absorb and reflect on your words, while also giving you a moment to collect your thoughts.

Mastering non-verbal communication is an ongoing process that requires practice and self-awareness. By paying attention to your body language, gestures, eye contact, facial expressions, and voice modulation, you can enhance your ability to connect with your audience and deliver a powerful speech on fear. Remember, non-verbal communication is a language of its own, and when used effectively, it can elevate your speaking skills to new heights.

Understanding Facial Expressions and Gestures

In the realm of public speaking, mastering the art of nonverbal communication is just as essential as delivering a well-crafted speech. Facial expressions and gestures are powerful tools that can significantly enhance your ability to convey your message with confidence and authenticity. By understanding the nuances of these nonverbal cues, you can conquer your fear and captivate any audience.

Facial expressions are the windows to our emotions. When we feel joy, sadness, anger, or fear, our face unconsciously reflects these emotions, providing valuable insights to those around us. As a speaker, being aware of your facial expressions can help you establish an immediate connection with your audience. A warm and genuine smile not only puts your listeners at ease but also signals your enthusiasm and passion for your topic.

Moreover, facial expressions can also be used strategically to emphasize specific points in your speech. Raising an eyebrow or furrowing your brow can convey surprise, skepticism, or curiosity, adding depth and intrigue to your delivery. By harnessing the power of facial expressions, you can effectively convey complex emotions and ideas, leaving a lasting impression on your audience.

Gestures, on the other hand, are physical movements that complement your spoken words. They can range from hand movements, nods, and head tilts, to body movements and posture shifts. By using gestures purposefully, you can enhance your verbal message, making it more engaging and memorable.

For instance, using open and expansive arm movements can convey confidence and authority, while small and delicate hand gestures can create a sense of intimacy and connection. However, it is essential to strike a balance and avoid excessive or distracting movements that may overshadow your speech. Practice your gestures to ensure they are smooth, natural, and in harmony with your message.

Understanding and utilizing facial expressions and gestures can also help you overcome your fear of public speaking. By paying attention to these nonverbal cues, you redirect your focus from your anxiety to effectively communicating your message. Embracing these tools empowers you to project confidence and control, gradually diminishing your fear and boosting your self-assurance as a speaker.

In conclusion, mastering the art of facial expressions and gestures is vital for any public speaker. By understanding the subtle nuances of nonverbal communication, you can establish a strong connection with your audience, emphasize key points, and conquer your fear of public speaking. With practice and self-awareness, you can harness the power of facial expressions and gestures to empower yourself and speak with confidence.

Utilizing Eye Contact for Connection

In the realm of public speaking, eye contact is an incredibly powerful tool. It has the ability to captivate an audience, establish trust, and create a deep connection between the speaker and the listeners. When it comes to conquering fear and empowering yourself to speak with confidence, mastering the art of eye contact is essential.

Eye contact is a universal language that transcends words. It allows you to connect with your audience on a deeper level, conveying your message not just through your words, but also through the sincerity and conviction in your eyes. It shows that you are present and engaged, and it encourages your listeners to do the same.

One of the key benefits of utilizing eye contact is the establishment of trust. When you maintain eye contact with your audience, it conveys a sense of honesty and authenticity. It shows that you are confident in what you are saying, and it encourages your audience to believe in you and your message. By establishing this trust, you create a safe space for your listeners, allowing them to be more receptive to your words.

Eye contact also helps to captivate your audience's attention. When you lock eyes with individuals in the crowd, they become more focused on you and what you have to say. It prevents their minds from wandering and keeps them engaged throughout your speech. By maintaining steady eye contact, you are able to hold their attention and ensure that your message is being received and understood.

Furthermore, eye contact allows you to establish a personal connection with your audience. By looking into someone's eyes, you acknowledge their presence and make them feel seen. This connection creates a sense of camaraderie and empathy, allowing your listeners to relate to you on a deeper level. It humanizes you as a speaker and makes your message more relatable and impactful.

In conclusion, utilizing eye contact is a powerful tool for connecting with your audience, conquering fear, and empowering yourself to speak with confidence. It establishes trust, captivates attention, and creates a personal connection. By mastering the art of eye contact, you can enhance the impact of your speeches and become a more effective communicator. So, next time you step on stage, remember the power of eye contact and embrace it as a means to connect with your listeners and leave a lasting impression.

In the realm of public speaking, eye contact is a powerful tool that can greatly enhance your ability to connect with your audience. The simple act of making eye contact can establish trust, build rapport, and create a sense of connection between speaker and listener. In this subchapter, we will explore the importance of eye contact and how it can empower you to conquer your fear of public speaking.

Eye contact is a fundamental aspect of human communication. When we look someone in the eye, it signals that we are present and engaged with them. As a speaker, making eye contact demonstrates your confidence and authenticity. It allows you to establish a personal connection with your audience, making them more receptive to your message.

One of the main benefits of utilizing eye contact is that it helps to overcome the fear of public speaking. When you make eye contact with individuals in the audience, it humanizes them and breaks down the barrier between speaker and listener. Instead of facing a sea of anonymous faces, you see individuals who are interested in what you have to say. This shift in perspective can help to alleviate anxiety and boost your confidence.

Furthermore, eye contact enables you to gauge the reactions of your audience. By looking into their eyes, you can observe their facial expressions and body language, allowing you to adjust your delivery accordingly. Are they engaged and nodding along? Or are they showing signs of confusion or disinterest? This real-time feedback can help you to adapt your speech and ensure that your message is effectively communicated.

To effectively utilize eye contact, it's important to maintain a balance. Avoid fixating on one person for too long, as it may make them uncomfortable. Instead, make brief eye contact with different individuals throughout the audience, ensuring that everyone feels included and acknowledged.

In conclusion, eye contact is a powerful tool that can empower you to conquer your fear of public speaking. By using eye contact to establish a connection with your audience, you can build trust, create rapport, and deliver your message with confidence. Remember to maintain a balance and make eye contact with various individuals throughout your speech. With practice, eye contact will become second nature, and you will find yourself speaking with greater confidence and impact.

Harnessing the Power of Voice and Tone

In the arena of public speaking, the impact of voice and tone cannot be underestimated. Whether you are addressing a small group or a large audience, the way you deliver your message can make or break your ability to conquer your fears and speak with confidence. Understanding how to harness the power of voice and tone is essential in becoming a truly effective and compelling speaker.

Voice is the vehicle through which your ideas are conveyed. It is the sound of your words, the pitch, volume, and rhythm that bring life to your message. Your voice should be a reflection of your inner confidence and conviction. It should resonate with authority and captivate your listeners. By mastering your voice, you can transform your fears into strengths.

One of the key aspects of voice is projection. In order to effectively communicate with a large audience, you must project your voice to ensure that everyone can hear you clearly. Take the time to practice and develop your vocal projection skills. Experiment with different techniques such as diaphragmatic breathing and vocal exercises to strengthen your voice and increase its reach.

Tone, on the other hand, is the emotional quality of your voice. It sets the mood and creates a connection with your audience. When speaking on the topic of fear, it is crucial to strike a balance between empathy and confidence. Your tone should reflect understanding and compassion, while also inspiring and motivating your listeners to overcome their own fears.

To harness the power of tone, pay attention to your intonation, inflection, and pacing. Varying your tone throughout your speech will prevent monotony and keep your audience engaged. Use pauses strategically to create suspense or highlight important points. Remember, your tone should be authentic and sincere, as it is the key to building trust and credibility with your audience.

In conclusion, the power of voice and tone cannot be underestimated in the realm of conquering fear and speaking with confidence. By mastering your voice and developing an effective tone, you can captivate your audience and inspire them to conquer their own fears. Take the time to practice and refine your vocal skills, and watch as your ability to connect with others and speak with confidence soars to new heights.

In the world of public speaking, the way you deliver your message is just as important as the content itself. Your voice and tone have the incredible ability to captivate an audience, evoke emotions, and convey confidence. When it comes to conquering fear and empowering yourself to speak with confidence, harnessing the power of voice and tone becomes indispensable.

Your voice is a unique instrument, capable of conveying a wide range of emotions and nuances. It is essential to recognize the impact your voice can have on your audience. By understanding how to use your voice effectively, you can influence and inspire others. The tone of your voice sets the emotional tone of your speech, allowing you to connect with your audience on a deeper level.

One crucial aspect of harnessing the power of voice and tone is understanding the importance of vocal variety. By varying your pitch, volume, and pace, you can add depth and interest to your speech. Experiment with different vocal techniques to create emphasis, highlight key points, and engage your audience. A monotone voice, on the other hand, can quickly lose your audience's attention and diminish the impact of your message.

Furthermore, being mindful of your tone is crucial. When speaking about fear, it is essential to strike a balance between empathy and encouragement. A warm and compassionate tone can help your audience feel understood and supported, while an overly aggressive or dismissive tone can alienate them. By adopting a tone that is both authoritative and approachable, you can establish credibility while creating a safe space for your audience to explore their fears.

Another element to consider is the power of pauses. Pausing strategically can enhance the impact of your words and allow your audience to reflect on your message. Pauses also provide you with a moment to collect your thoughts and maintain control over your nerves. Embrace the silence and use it to your advantage.

In summary, harnessing the power of voice and tone is vital in conquering fear and empowering yourself to speak with confidence. By understanding how to use your voice effectively, varying your tone, and embracing strategic pauses, you can create a truly impactful speech on fear. Remember, your voice is a powerful tool, capable of inspiring and influencing others. Embrace its potential and let it guide you on your journey to conquering fear and speaking with confidence.

Chapter 4: Practicing and Preparing for Public Speaking

Creating Engaging Content

In today's fast-paced digital world, capturing and maintaining the attention of your audience is more challenging than ever. Whether you are delivering a speech on fear or any other topic, creating engaging content is essential to keep your audience interested and involved. This subchapter will provide you with valuable insights and practical tips to help you create captivating and impactful speeches that will leave a lasting impression on your listeners.

The key to creating engaging content lies in understanding your audience. Every individual has unique preferences and interests. Therefore, it is crucial to research and analyze your target audience to tailor your content accordingly. By doing so, you can identify their needs, concerns, and desires, allowing you to connect with them on a deeper level.

One effective strategy to engage your audience is through storytelling. Stories have a way of captivating people's attention and evoking emotions. By incorporating personal anecdotes or relatable narratives into your speech on fear, you can make your content more relatable and memorable. Additionally, using vivid language and descriptive details will help paint a vivid picture in the minds of your listeners, making your content more engaging.

Another tip to create engaging content is to incorporate interactive elements. People are more likely to retain information and stay engaged when they actively participate. Consider incorporating activities, group discussions, or Q&A sessions into your speech on fear. This will not only keep your audience engaged but also encourage active learning and participation.

Utilizing multimedia elements can also make your content more engaging. Visual aids such as slideshows, videos, or infographics can help illustrate your points and add variety to your speech. Be mindful, however, not to overload your presentation with too many visuals, as this can distract from your message.

Lastly, remember that engaging content is not just about the delivery but also about authenticity. Be genuine and passionate about your topic. Your enthusiasm will be infectious and will spark interest and engagement from your audience.

Creating engaging content requires careful planning, research, and creativity. By understanding your audience, incorporating storytelling, interactive elements, multimedia, and maintaining authenticity, you can captivate your audience's attention and deliver a powerful speech on fear that will empower and inspire every individual in the room.

When it comes to delivering a speech on fear, it is crucial to capture the attention and engage your audience. Creating engaging content not only helps your message resonate with your listeners but also leaves a lasting impact. In this subchapter, we will explore various strategies and techniques to help you create captivating content that empowers you to speak with confidence.

One of the most effective ways to engage your audience is by sharing personal stories and experiences related to fear. Think about a time when you faced your fears and overcame them. By sharing these stories, you not only connect with your audience on a deeper level but also inspire them to confront their own fears. Remember to be authentic and vulnerable as this will make your speech relatable and memorable.

Another essential aspect of creating engaging content is appealing to the emotions of your audience. Fear is a powerful emotion, and by leveraging it in your speech, you can evoke strong feelings within your listeners. Use descriptive language and vivid imagery to paint a picture of the fear you are discussing. Additionally, incorporating humor can help alleviate tension and keep your audience engaged throughout your speech.

To further enhance engagement, consider using multimedia elements in your presentation. Visual aids such as images, videos, or slides can complement your spoken words and provide a visual representation of fear. They can also serve as a break from the monotony of listening, capturing attention and reinforcing your message.

Furthermore, incorporating interactive elements into your speech can significantly increase engagement. Encourage audience participation through activities, questions, or discussions. This not only keeps your listeners actively involved but also allows them to reflect on their own fears and share their thoughts and experiences.

Lastly, remember the importance of structuring your content effectively. Begin with a strong opening that hooks your audience's attention, followed by a clear introduction of the topic. Then, organize your main points in a logical and coherent manner, ensuring a smooth flow from one idea to the next. Finally, conclude your speech with a powerful and memorable ending that leaves your listeners inspired and motivated to conquer their own fears.

In conclusion, creating engaging content for a speech on fear is essential to capture your audience's attention and empower them to confront their fears. By sharing personal stories, appealing to emotions, incorporating multimedia elements, encouraging participation, and structuring your content effectively, you can deliver a compelling speech that resonates with every individual in the room. Remember, it is through engaging content that you will conquer your own fear of public speaking and inspire others to do the same.

Structuring Your Speech

The ability to deliver a powerful and impactful speech is a skill that can be developed by anyone. Whether you are addressing a large audience or speaking one-on-one, structuring your speech effectively is vital to engage your listeners and convey your message with confidence. In this subchapter, we will explore some key strategies for structuring a speech specifically focused on the topic of fear, enabling you to conquer your fears and empower yourself as a speaker.

1. Start with a captivating introduction: Begin your speech by grabbing your audience's attention and setting the stage for your message. Consider using a compelling anecdote, a surprising statistic, or a thought-provoking question related to fear. This will immediately captivate your listeners and make them eager to hear more.

2. Clearly define your purpose: Clearly articulate the purpose of your speech, which is to address the topic of fear. Whether you aim to educate, inspire, or motivate your audience, make your intention explicit from the start. This will help your listeners understand the relevance of your speech and engage with your message more effectively.

3. Organize your content logically: Structure your speech into distinct sections or points to ensure clarity and coherence. For instance, you can divide your speech on fear into segments such as the causes of fear, the effects of fear, and strategies to overcome fear. This logical organization will help your audience follow your ideas seamlessly.

4. Use storytelling techniques: Incorporate personal anecdotes or stories to illustrate your points and make your speech relatable.

Sharing your own experiences with fear and how you overcame them will create a connection with your audience, making your message more impactful and memorable.

5. Provide evidence and examples: Support your ideas with credible evidence, such as expert opinions or research studies, to enhance the credibility of your speech. Additionally, use real-life examples to illustrate your points and make them more tangible for your audience.

6. Conclude with a call to action: Wrap up your speech by summarizing your key points and leaving your audience with a call to action. Encourage them to take steps towards conquering their fears, whether it is seeking professional help, setting small achievable goals, or practicing self-compassion. This will empower your listeners to take action and apply what they have learned from your speech.

In summary, structuring your speech effectively is crucial to deliver a powerful message on the topic of fear. By captivating your audience from the beginning, organizing your content logically, incorporating personal stories, providing evidence, and concluding with a call to action, you will empower yourself to speak with confidence and inspire others to conquer their fears as well.

When it comes to giving a speech, proper structure is essential for effectively conveying your message and engaging your audience. This is especially important when addressing the topic of fear, as it can be an intense and sensitive subject for many individuals. In this subchapter, we will explore various techniques and strategies to help you structure your speech on fear in a way that empowers and resonates with your audience.

1.   Introduction:

Begin your speech with a strong and attention-grabbing opening. Consider sharing a personal anecdote or a thought-provoking quote to establish a connection with your audience. Clearly state the purpose of your speech and why the topic of fear is important to discuss.

2.   Body:

The body of your speech should be well-organized and coherent. Divide it into several key points or subtopics, each with its own supporting evidence or examples. Explore different aspects of fear, such as its causes, effects, and ways to overcome it. Use storytelling techniques to make your speech relatable and engaging.

3.   Addressing   the   Audience's   Concerns:

Acknowledge that fear is a universal experience and emphasize that your speech is a safe space for everyone to share their feelings. Address common concerns and doubts that your audience may have about facing their fears. Provide reassurance and practical advice on how to navigate through fear and move towards personal empowerment.

4.   Visual   Aids   and   Props:

Consider incorporating visual aids and props to enhance your speech. Images, graphs, or videos can help illustrate your points and create a more impactful experience for your audience. Props, such as objects symbolizing different fears, can serve as powerful visual reminders of the topic at hand.

5.   Conclusion:

End your speech on a strong note by summarizing your main points and reinforcing your message of empowerment. Leave your audience with a call to action, encouraging them to confront their fears and take steps towards personal growth. Consider ending with an inspiring quote or a memorable story to leave a lasting impression.

Remember, structuring your speech is crucial, but it is equally important to practice and rehearse your delivery. Pay attention to your body language, tone of voice, and pacing to ensure that your message is effectively conveyed. With a well-structured speech and confident delivery, you can inspire and empower your audience to conquer their fears and speak with confidence.

Crafting Captivating Introductions and Conclusions

Introduction:

The ability to captivate an audience from the very beginning of your speech is essential for effective communication. Introductions not only set the tone for your presentation but also allow you to establish a connection with your listeners. Similarly, conclusions provide a lasting impression, leaving your audience with a powerful takeaway. In this subchapter, we will explore the art of crafting captivating introductions and conclusions, specifically tailored to speeches on fear. Whether you are a seasoned speaker or someone who struggles with public speaking, these techniques will empower you to speak with confidence and conquer your fear.

Crafting Captivating Introductions:

1. Start with a compelling anecdote: Begin your speech with a personal story or a relatable experience that illustrates the impact of fear. This will instantly grab your audience's attention and make them eager to hear more.

2. Use a powerful quote: Incorporate a relevant and thought-provoking quote that encapsulates the essence of fear. Quotes from renowned individuals who have overcome fear can inspire and resonate with your audience.

3. Pose a rhetorical question: Engage your listeners by asking a question that challenges their perception of fear. This will encourage them to reflect on their own fears and create an atmosphere of curiosity.

4. Utilize vivid imagery: Paint a picture with words by using descriptive language that evokes strong emotions. This will help your audience visualize the fear you are discussing and create a stronger connection.

Crafting Impactful Conclusions:

1. Revisit the introduction: Refer back to your captivating introduction to remind your audience of the journey you have taken them on. This will create a sense of closure and reinforce the key points you have made.

2. Provide a call to action: Inspire your audience to take action by suggesting practical steps they can implement to overcome their fears. By offering tangible solutions, you empower them to make a positive change in their lives.

3. End with a memorable quote: Leave your audience with a lasting impression by concluding your speech with a powerful quote that encapsulates the essence of overcoming fear. This will resonate with your listeners long after your speech has ended.

Conclusion:

Crafting captivating introductions and conclusions is an art that can significantly enhance the impact of your speeches on fear. By incorporating personal anecdotes, powerful quotes, rhetorical questions, and vivid imagery, you can engage your audience from the start. Similarly, revisiting the introduction, providing a call to action, and concluding with a memorable quote can leave a lasting impression. Remember, conquering your fear of public speaking is not only about delivering a powerful message, but also about connecting with your audience. With these techniques, you can confidently empower yourself to speak with conviction and inspire others to overcome their fears.

Introduction:

The power of a well-crafted introduction and conclusion cannot be underestimated when it comes to delivering a speech on fear. These crucial moments set the tone for your entire presentation and have the ability to captivate your audience right from the start. In this subchapter, we will explore the art of crafting captivating introductions and conclusions, empowering you to speak with confidence and make a lasting impact.

Captivating Introductions:

1. Start with a compelling anecdote or personal story that relates to the topic of fear. By sharing a relatable experience, you immediately grab the attention of your audience and create a connection.

2. Pose a thought-provoking question that challenges your listeners to think about their own fears and how they can overcome them. This engages their minds and encourages active participation.

3. Utilize a powerful quote or statistic that highlights the significance of fear in our lives. This not only adds credibility to your speech but also creates a sense of urgency and intrigue.

4. Begin with a startling fact or surprising statement that immediately grabs attention. This can be an effective way to pique curiosity and make your audience eager to hear more.

Crafting Memorable Conclusions:

1. Summarize your main points and reinforce the key message of your speech. By restating your main ideas, you ensure that your audience leaves with a clear understanding of what you wanted to convey.

2. End with a call to action, encouraging your listeners to take steps towards conquering their fears. By providing tangible steps or resources, you empower them to make positive changes in their lives.

3. Use a powerful and inspiring quote that resonates with your audience. This can leave a lasting impression and inspire them to reflect on their own fears long after your speech is over.

4. Finish with an impactful story or anecdote that ties back to the theme of fear. By leaving your audience with a memorable story, you ensure that they will remember your speech and the lessons it taught.

Conclusion:

Crafting captivating introductions and conclusions is an art form that can significantly enhance the impact of your speech on fear. By employing techniques such as sharing personal stories, asking thought-provoking questions, and utilizing powerful quotes, you can immediately engage your audience and create a lasting impression. Additionally, by summarizing your main points, providing a call to action, and ending with a memorable anecdote, you ensure that your audience leaves with a clear understanding and a newfound motivation to conquer their fears. With these tools in hand, you are now empowered to speak with confidence and inspire others to overcome their fears as well.

Utilizing Persuasive Techniques in Your Speech

In the realm of public speaking, the ability to persuade and influence your audience is a powerful skill to possess. Whether you are addressing a small group or a large audience, mastering persuasive techniques in your speech can help you convey your message effectively and leave a lasting impact on your listeners. This subchapter aims to equip you with the tools necessary to harness the power of persuasion and conquer your fear of public speaking.

One of the most crucial aspects of persuasive speaking is establishing credibility. Your audience needs to perceive you as a knowledgeable and trustworthy speaker. To achieve this, it is imperative to conduct thorough research on your topic and present well-supported facts and evidence. Additionally, sharing personal experiences and anecdotes can help build a connection with your listeners and make your speech more relatable.

Another effective technique is to appeal to your audience's emotions. Fear is a universal emotion, and by tapping into this emotion, you can create a sense of empathy and urgency. Share stories that evoke emotions related to fear, but also provide practical solutions or inspiring examples that offer hope and encouragement. This will enable your audience to see that fear can be overcome and motivate them to take action.

Using persuasive language is also essential in capturing your audience's attention and maintaining their interest. Employ rhetorical devices such as repetition, alliteration, and metaphors to make your speech more engaging and memorable. Additionally, employing the power of positive language can inspire and uplift your listeners, making them more receptive to your message.

Furthermore, incorporating visual aids can enhance the persuasive impact of your speech. Utilize images, graphs, and videos to support your arguments and make complex information more accessible. Visual aids not only enhance comprehension but also create a lasting impression on your audience.

Lastly, mastering the art of effective storytelling can significantly enhance your persuasive speaking skills. Humans are naturally drawn to stories, and weaving your message into a compelling narrative can captivate your audience's attention and make your speech more persuasive. Craft narratives that highlight the journey from fear to empowerment, emphasizing the transformative power of conquering fear.

In conclusion, by utilizing persuasive techniques in your speech, you can conquer your fear of public speaking and empower yourself to deliver impactful messages. Establishing credibility, appealing to emotions, using persuasive language, incorporating visual aids, and storytelling are all essential tools to engage and persuade your audience. Embrace these techniques, practice them diligently, and watch as your speeches become more persuasive and influential. Remember, with determination and practice, your fear of public speaking can be conquered, and your voice can be a powerful force for change.

In the realm of public speaking, the ability to persuade your audience is an invaluable tool. Whether you are delivering a speech on overcoming fear or any other topic, employing persuasive techniques can help you effectively convey your message and leave a lasting impact on your listeners. By mastering these techniques, you can empower yourself to speak with confidence and inspire others to conquer their own fears.

One of the most powerful persuasive techniques is storytelling. Humans are naturally drawn to narratives, and by incorporating personal anecdotes or relatable stories into your speech, you can captivate your audience's attention and create an emotional connection. By sharing your own experiences of overcoming fear, you can demonstrate that it is possible to conquer even the most daunting challenges, inspiring your listeners to do the same.

Another effective technique is the use of rhetorical questions. By posing thought-provoking questions to your audience, you can engage them in a deeper level of reflection and encourage active participation. This not only helps to sustain their attention, but also allows them to consider their own fears and contemplate potential solutions. By guiding them through this introspective process, you can motivate them to take action and face their fears head-on.

Additionally, the strategic use of evidence and statistics can lend credibility to your speech. People are more likely to be persuaded by factual information, so incorporating relevant data and research into your arguments can strengthen your position and make your message more convincing. By presenting concrete evidence that supports your claims, you can overcome skepticism and build trust with your audience.

Furthermore, the power of repetition cannot be underestimated. By reiterating key points throughout your speech, you reinforce your message and ensure that it resonates with your listeners. Additionally, employing powerful and vivid language can evoke strong emotions, making your speech more memorable and impactful.

In conclusion, when delivering a speech on fear or any other topic, utilizing persuasive techniques can greatly enhance your ability to connect with your audience and inspire them to take action. By integrating storytelling, rhetorical questions, evidence, repetition, and powerful language into your speech, you can empower yourself to speak with confidence and conquer your own fears. Remember, the aim is not only to inform but also to persuade, so make use of these techniques to create a speech that truly resonates with your audience, leaving a lasting impression and inspiring positive change.

Overcoming Stage Fright

Stage fright, also known as performance anxiety, is a common fear that many individuals experience when they are required to speak in front of a group. Whether it is giving a presentation at work, delivering a speech at a wedding, or performing on stage, the fear of being judged or making a mistake can be paralyzing. However, it is important to remember that stage fright is not something that should hold you back from expressing yourself.

In this subchapter, we will explore effective strategies to overcome stage fright and empower yourself to speak with confidence. These techniques can be applied to any situation where fear and anxiety may hinder your ability to deliver a speech or perform in front of an audience.

One of the most effective ways to overcome stage fright is through preparation and practice. By thoroughly familiarizing yourself with the content of your speech or performance, you will gain confidence in your abilities. Practice in front of a mirror or with a trusted friend or family member, and gradually increase the size of your audience as you become more comfortable.

Another useful technique is to reframe your mindset. Instead of viewing the situation as a high-stakes performance, shift your perspective to see it as an opportunity to share your knowledge or passion with others. Remember that your audience wants you to succeed and is rooting for you.

Deep breathing exercises and relaxation techniques can also help alleviate anxiety. Take a few moments before your speech or performance to focus on your breath and visualize yourself succeeding. This will help calm your nerves and improve your overall performance.

Additionally, it can be helpful to engage with your audience. Make eye contact, smile, and use gestures to connect with them. This will not only make you feel more at ease but also create a positive and engaging experience for your listeners.

Lastly, it is crucial to remember that overcoming stage fright takes time and practice. Be patient with yourself and celebrate small victories along the way. Each time you successfully deliver a speech or perform in front of an audience, you are one step closer to conquering your fear.

In conclusion, stage fright is a common fear that many individuals experience when speaking in front of an audience. However, by employing strategies such as preparation, reframing your mindset, practicing relaxation techniques, engaging with your audience, and being patient with yourself, you can overcome stage fright and speak with confidence. Remember, you have valuable ideas and perspectives to share, and the world deserves to hear your voice.

Stage fright, also known as performance anxiety, is a common fear that many individuals experience when speaking in public. Whether it's giving a presentation at work, delivering a speech at a social gathering, or performing on a stage, the fear of being judged or making mistakes can be overwhelming. However, it is important to understand that stage fright is a natural response and can be overcome with the right strategies and mindset.

In this subchapter, we will explore effective techniques to conquer stage fright and empower yourself to speak with confidence. These techniques are applicable to everyone, regardless of their experience level or the specific niche of their speech.

1. Preparation is Key: One of the most effective ways to combat stage fright is to thoroughly prepare for your speech. Research your topic, organize your thoughts, and rehearse your delivery. The more confident you feel about your content, the less anxious you will be on stage.

2. Visualization and Positive Affirmations: Visualize yourself delivering a successful and engaging speech. Imagine the audience being captivated by your words and applauding your performance. Additionally, repeat positive affirmations to yourself such as "I am confident" or "I am a skilled public speaker." These techniques can help boost your self-belief and reduce anxiety.

3. Deep Breathing and Relaxation Techniques: Before stepping on stage, practice deep breathing exercises to calm your nerves. Inhale deeply through your nose, hold it for a few seconds, and then exhale slowly through your mouth. You can also incorporate other relaxation techniques such as progressive muscle relaxation or meditation to alleviate anxiety.

4. Focus on the Audience: Instead of fixating on your own fears and insecurities, shift your focus to the audience. Remember that they are there to listen and learn from you. Engage with them, make eye contact, and connect with their energy. This shift in focus can help

redirect nervous energy into a more positive and confident performance.

5. Embrace Imperfections: Understand that making mistakes is a part of the learning process. Even the most seasoned speakers stumble or forget their lines at times. Embrace imperfections and view them as opportunities to grow. Learn to laugh at yourself and keep moving forward.

Remember, stage fright is a common experience shared by many. By implementing these strategies and adopting a positive mindset, you can conquer your fear and speak with confidence. Embrace the challenge, believe in yourself, and watch your public speaking skills soar to new heights.

Fear of public speaking is a common phobia that affects people from all walks of life. Whether you are a seasoned professional or a student preparing for a class presentation, stage fright can strike anyone at any time. However, with the right strategies and mindset, you can conquer your fear and speak with confidence. In this subchapter, we will explore effective techniques to help you overcome stage fright and deliver powerful speeches on fear.

1. Understand the root cause: The first step in overcoming stage fright is to understand where it stems from. Fear of judgment, rejection, or failure often underlies stage fright. Recognize that these fears are natural but can be overcome with practice and self-belief.

2. Preparation is key: One of the most effective ways to combat stage fright is thorough preparation. Research your topic extensively, organize your thoughts, and practice your speech multiple times. The

more familiar you are with your material, the more confident you will feel on stage.

3. Visualization exercises: Visualizing success can be a powerful tool in overcoming stage fright. Close your eyes and imagine yourself delivering a flawless speech, receiving applause, and feeling confident. This mental rehearsal can help boost your self-assurance and reduce anxiety.

4. Breathing and relaxation techniques: Deep breathing exercises can help calm your nerves before and during a speech. Take slow, deep breaths to relax your body and mind. Additionally, incorporating relaxation techniques such as meditation or yoga into your daily routine can help manage overall anxiety.

5. Start small: Begin by speaking in front of a smaller and more supportive audience, such as friends or family. Gradually increase the size of your audience while maintaining a positive mindset. Each successful experience will build your confidence and diminish your stage fright.

6. Embrace your nervous energy: Instead of viewing your nervousness as a weakness, reframe it as excitement. Understand that the adrenaline and butterflies you feel are signs that you care about your message. Embrace this energy and use it to your advantage to deliver a passionate speech.

7. Seek professional help if needed: If your stage fright is severe and significantly impacts your daily life, consider seeking professional help. Therapists or public speaking coaches can provide valuable guidance and techniques tailored to your specific needs.

Remember, overcoming stage fright is a journey that takes time and practice. By implementing these strategies and maintaining a positive mindset, you can gradually conquer your fear and become a confident speaker on the topic of fear. Embrace the opportunity to empower yourself and inspire others with your words.

Breathing Exercises for Relaxation

In the journey of conquering fear and empowering yourself to speak with confidence, one key aspect that often gets overlooked is the power of breath. Our breath is not only essential for survival but also holds the potential to calm our minds and bodies, allowing us to overcome fear and anxiety. This subchapter delves into the practice of breathing exercises for relaxation, providing you with effective techniques to incorporate into your preparation for speeches on fear.

Breathing exercises are simple yet powerful tools that can be practiced by anyone, regardless of their experience or expertise. By focusing on the breath, we can activate the body's relaxation response, counteracting the fight-or-flight response triggered by fear. These exercises help in slowing down our heart rate, reducing muscle tension, and calming the mind.

One of the most common and effective techniques is diaphragmatic breathing, also known as belly breathing. To practice this exercise, sit or lie down in a comfortable position. Place one hand on your chest and the other on your abdomen. Inhale deeply through your nose, allowing your belly to rise as you fill your lungs with air. Exhale slowly through your mouth, feeling your belly descend. Repeat this process for a few minutes, focusing on the sensation of your breath and letting go of any tension or worry.

Another technique is the 4-7-8 breathing exercise, which helps regulate breathing and induce a state of relaxation. Start by inhaling silently through your nose to a mental count of four. Hold your breath for a count of seven. Exhale completely through your mouth to a count of eight, making a whooshing sound. This exercise can be repeated up to four times, ideally twice a day.

In addition to these techniques, alternate nostril breathing and box breathing are also beneficial practices to explore. The former involves closing one nostril with your finger while inhaling, then switching nostrils while exhaling. The latter involves inhaling for a count of four, holding for four, exhaling for four, and holding again for four.

By incorporating these breathing exercises into your daily routine, you can cultivate a sense of calm and relaxation, empowering yourself to speak with confidence. Remember that practice is key, and the more you dedicate yourself to these exercises, the more effective they will become in managing fear and anxiety.

Now that you have discovered the power of breathing exercises for relaxation, take some time each day to prioritize your mental well-being. By harnessing the strength of your breath, you can conquer fear, find your voice, and deliver speeches on fear with confidence.

In the journey of conquering fear and empowering yourself to speak with confidence, it is essential to recognize the power of relaxation techniques. One of the most effective and accessible methods to calm your nerves and steady your mind is through breathing exercises. By incorporating simple breathing techniques into your daily routine, you can cultivate a state of relaxation that will help you combat your fear of public speaking and deliver impactful speeches.

Deep abdominal breathing is a fundamental exercise that can be practiced anywhere, at any time. Start by finding a quiet space and sitting or lying down in a comfortable position. Place one hand on your chest and the other on your abdomen. Inhale slowly through your nose, allowing your abdomen to rise as you fill your lungs with air. Exhale gradually through your mouth, feeling your abdomen sink as you release the breath. Focus on the sensation of your breath entering and leaving your body, allowing any tension or anxiety to melt away with each exhale. Repeat this cycle for a few minutes, gradually lengthening your breaths as you become more comfortable.

Another beneficial breathing exercise is the 4-7-8 technique. Close your eyes and take a deep breath in through your nose for a count of four. Hold your breath for a count of seven, and then exhale slowly through your mouth for a count of eight. This technique helps to regulate your breath, calm your nervous system, and induce a state of relaxation.

Box breathing, also known as square breathing, is a method used by many to combat anxiety and stress. Visualize a square in your mind. Inhale deeply for a count of four as you trace the first side of the square. Hold your breath for a count of four as you trace the second side. Exhale slowly for a count of four as you trace the third side. Finally, hold your breath for a count of four as you complete the square. Repeat this pattern for several rounds, allowing your body and mind to unwind.

Incorporating these breathing exercises into your daily routine will not only help you manage your fear of public speaking but also enhance your overall well-being. By practicing these techniques regularly, you will develop a greater sense of calm, control, and confidence, enabling you to deliver speeches with poise and clarity. Remember, everyone can benefit from these exercises, regardless of their niche or experience in public speaking. Start today and experience the transformative power of relaxation through breathing.

In the journey of conquering fear and empowering yourself to speak with confidence, it is crucial to incorporate relaxation techniques into your routine. One such technique that can work wonders is practicing breathing exercises. These exercises not only calm your mind and body but also help in combating the physical symptoms of fear and anxiety that often accompany public speaking.

For centuries, various cultures have recognized the power of conscious breathing. By focusing on your breath, you can bring yourself to the present moment, release tension, and create a sense of calm within. The beauty of breathing exercises is that they can be practiced anytime and anywhere, making them a convenient tool to have in your arsenal.

One effective breathing exercise that can aid in relaxation is the 4-7-8 technique. Begin by finding a quiet place where you can sit comfortably. Close your eyes and inhale deeply through your nose for a count of four. Hold your breath for a count of seven, and then exhale slowly through your mouth for a count of eight. Repeat this cycle for at least four rounds, focusing on the sensation of your breath entering and leaving your body. This exercise helps activate the body's relaxation response, inducing a deep sense of calm.

Another technique to consider is diaphragmatic breathing, also known as belly breathing. Place one hand on your chest and the other on your abdomen. Take a slow, deep breath in through your nose, allowing your abdomen to rise as you fill your lungs with air. Exhale slowly through your mouth, feeling your abdomen fall. Practice this technique for a few minutes every day, gradually increasing the duration. Diaphragmatic breathing helps regulate your breathing pattern, promoting relaxation and reducing anxiety.

Remember, these exercises are not a quick fix but rather a skill that requires practice. Incorporating them into your daily routine will enhance your ability to manage fear and anxiety associated with public speaking. As you become more proficient in these techniques, you will notice an improvement in your overall speaking confidence.

Breathing exercises are a valuable tool for everyone, regardless of their niche or area of expertise. Whether you are an experienced speaker or someone just starting to overcome their fear of public speaking, implementing these techniques can significantly contribute to your success. So, take a few moments each day to focus on your breath, and witness the transformation it brings to your mindset and performance.

Visualizing Success

In the realm of public speaking, fear is a common enemy that can hold us back from reaching our full potential. It paralyzes us, making it difficult to express our thoughts and ideas with confidence. However, by conquering fear, we can empower ourselves to become effective speakers who captivate audiences and deliver impactful messages.

One powerful technique that can help us overcome fear and boost our confidence is the practice of visualizing success. Visualization is a tool used by many successful individuals, from athletes to entrepreneurs, to enhance performance and achieve their goals. By harnessing the power of our minds, we can create a mental image of ourselves delivering a speech with confidence, poise, and clarity.

When we visualize success, we create a mental movie in which we see ourselves standing on stage, speaking eloquently, and connecting effortlessly with our audience. We imagine the positive reactions from our listeners, the applause, and the sense of accomplishment that comes from delivering a powerful speech. By repeatedly visualizing these scenarios, we begin to rewire our subconscious mind, replacing fear and self-doubt with confidence and self-assurance.

To effectively visualize success, it is essential to create a clear and vivid mental image. Close your eyes and imagine the details of the scene – the stage, the lights, the faces of the audience members. Hear your own voice, strong and steady, resonating throughout the room. Feel the confidence radiating from within as you deliver each word with conviction.

In addition to visualizing the end result, it is important to visualize the process of preparation. See yourself dedicating time to research and practice, becoming an expert in your topic. Visualize yourself rehearsing your speech, feeling the words flow naturally from your lips. By visualizing the steps leading up to your success, you will reinforce the belief that you have what it takes to conquer your fear and deliver an outstanding speech.

Remember, visualization alone is not enough – it must be accompanied by action. Use your visualization practice as a motivator to take tangible steps towards improving your speaking skills. Seek opportunities to speak in front of others, join public speaking clubs, or enroll in courses that will enhance your communication abilities. By combining visualization with action, you will be well on your way to conquering fear and becoming a confident and influential speaker.

In conclusion, visualizing success is a powerful technique that can empower individuals to overcome their fear of public speaking. By creating a clear mental image of ourselves delivering a speech with confidence and connecting with our audience, we can reprogram our subconscious mind and replace fear with self-assurance. However, visualization alone is not enough – it must be accompanied by action and a commitment to continuous improvement. By incorporating both visualization and action into our journey, we can conquer our fear, empower ourselves, and speak with confidence.

In the journey of conquering fear and empowering yourself to speak with confidence, one powerful tool that can significantly contribute to your success is the practice of visualizing success. Visualizing success involves creating vivid mental images of yourself confidently delivering a speech, overcoming your fear, and achieving your desired outcomes. This subchapter will explore the importance of visualizing success and provide practical tips on how to incorporate this technique into your speech on fear.

Visualizing success is a proven technique used by athletes, performers, and successful individuals from various fields. It taps into the power of the mind to create a positive mindset and enhance self-belief. When you visualize success, you are programming your subconscious mind to focus on achieving your goals and reinforcing positive thought patterns.

In the context of delivering a speech on fear, visualizing success can be a game-changer. By visualizing yourself confidently and smoothly delivering your speech, you are rewiring your brain to believe in your abilities and overcome any fear or anxiety. It allows you to mentally rehearse the speech, anticipate potential challenges, and develop strategies to overcome them.

To incorporate visualizing success into your speech on fear, start by finding a quiet and comfortable space where you can relax and focus. Close your eyes and imagine yourself standing on the stage, feeling calm and confident. Visualize the audience engaged and attentive, hanging onto your every word. Picture yourself speaking with clarity, poise, and conviction, radiating confidence and authority.

As you visualize, engage all your senses. Feel the sensation of standing tall, breathing deeply, and projecting your voice. Hear the applause and encouraging feedback from the audience. Smell the air in the room and observe the positive energy surrounding you. The more detailed and vivid your visualizations, the more powerful their impact will be.

Additionally, it can be helpful to create a vision board or a collage of images that represent your desired success. Place this visual representation in a prominent location where you can see it daily. This will serve as a constant reminder of your goals and reinforce your commitment to conquering your fear.

Remember, visualizing success is not a one-time exercise but a continuous practice. Regularly spend time visualizing your success, especially before important speaking engagements. With consistent effort, you will gradually reprogram your mind, boost your confidence, and overcome your fear of public speaking.

In conclusion, visualizing success is a valuable technique that can empower you to speak with confidence and conquer your fear. By harnessing the power of your mind and creating positive mental images, you can transform your anxieties into strengths. Incorporate visualizing success into your speech on fear and witness the remarkable difference it makes in your journey to becoming a confident and effective speaker.

In the journey of conquering fear and empowering oneself to speak with confidence, one powerful tool that can be utilized is the art of visualizing success. Visualization is a technique that allows individuals to create mental images of themselves achieving their goals and succeeding in their endeavors. By visualizing success, individuals can effectively overcome their fear of speaking and develop the confidence needed to deliver impactful speeches.

Visualization is a technique that can be used by everyone, regardless of their level of expertise or experience in public speaking. It is a simple yet effective way to reprogram the mind and build self-assurance. By visualizing success, individuals can create a positive mental state, which is essential for overcoming fear and anxiety. When one can vividly imagine themselves delivering a speech flawlessly, with confidence and poise, it becomes easier to believe in their own abilities.

To begin visualizing success, it is important to find a quiet and comfortable space where one can relax and focus. Close your eyes and take a few deep breaths, allowing your body to relax and your mind to calm. Picture yourself standing on a stage, in front of an audience, ready to deliver your speech. Visualize the audience engaged and captivated by your words, nodding in agreement, and applauding your performance.

As you continue to visualize, focus on the details of your success. Imagine yourself speaking with a clear and confident voice, making eye contact with the audience, and using gestures to emphasize key points. Visualize the positive reactions from the audience, the sense of accomplishment, and the feeling of empowerment that comes with conquering your fear.

It is important to practice visualization regularly, ideally on a daily basis. By consistently visualizing success, you are training your mind to believe in your abilities and to overcome any self-doubt or fear that may arise. The more vividly you can imagine your success, the more likely it is to become a reality.

In conclusion, visualizing success is a powerful technique that can greatly assist individuals in conquering their fear and speaking with confidence. By creating mental images of success, individuals can reprogram their minds to believe in their abilities and overcome their fear of speaking. Regular practice of visualization can lead to increased self-assurance, improved public speaking skills, and ultimately, the empowerment to speak confidently in any situation.

Rehearsing and Practicing Your Speech

One of the most effective ways to overcome your fear of public speaking is to rehearse and practice your speech thoroughly. Rehearsing allows you to become familiar with the content and flow of your speech, while practicing helps you gain confidence and control over your delivery. Whether you are giving a speech on fear or any other topic, the following tips will help you conquer your fear and speak with confidence.

Firstly, start by breaking down your speech into smaller sections or key points. This will make it easier to memorize and deliver your speech in a more organized manner. Make sure you have a clear understanding of each point and how they connect to one another. Practice delivering each section individually until you feel comfortable with it, and then gradually start combining them.

Next, consider recording yourself while rehearsing your speech. This can be done using your smartphone or any other recording device. By listening to your recordings, you will be able to identify areas where you need improvement, such as pacing, clarity, or body language. It also helps you become more aware of any nervous habits or filler words that you may need to eliminate.

Furthermore, try to simulate the actual speaking environment during your practice sessions. Stand up, use a podium or microphone if possible, and imagine yourself speaking in front of an audience. This will help you become more accustomed to the physicality of public speaking. Additionally, practice with a friend or family member who can provide feedback and constructive criticism.

In addition to practicing the words of your speech, pay attention to your non-verbal communication. Practice maintaining eye contact, using appropriate gestures, and controlling your body language. Remember that your body language can greatly influence how your message is perceived by the audience.

Lastly, don't forget to practice managing your nerves. Incorporate relaxation techniques such as deep breathing exercises, visualization, or meditation into your rehearsal routine. These techniques can help calm your nerves and increase your overall confidence.

In conclusion, rehearsing and practicing your speech is essential for conquering your fear and speaking with confidence. Break down your speech into smaller sections, record yourself for self-assessment, simulate the speaking environment, and focus on non-verbal communication. By incorporating these tips into your preparation, you will be better equipped to deliver a powerful and confident speech on fear or any other topic. Remember, practice makes perfect!

One of the most effective ways to overcome the fear of public speaking is through thorough preparation and practice. In this subchapter, we will discuss the importance of rehearsing and practicing your speech to empower yourself and speak with confidence. Whether you are delivering a speech on fear or any other topic, these tips will help you conquer your fear and deliver a compelling presentation.

To begin, it is crucial to allocate ample time for preparation. Set aside dedicated blocks of time to plan and structure your speech. Start by identifying your main points and supporting evidence. Craft a clear and concise message that resonates with your audience. Remember, the more you understand your topic and have a well-organized speech, the more confident you will feel when delivering it.

Once you have outlined your speech, it's time to start rehearsing. Practice your speech out loud, ideally in front of a mirror or a supportive friend. This will help you refine your delivery, body language, and gestures. Pay attention to your voice tone, pitch, and pace. Practice breathing exercises to manage any anxiety or nervousness that may arise.

Additionally, consider recording yourself during practice sessions. This allows you to review your performance objectively and identify areas for improvement. Listen to your recordings carefully, paying attention to clarity, pronunciation, and overall confidence. Use this feedback to adjust your speech and focus on areas that need more attention.

Furthermore, consider joining a public speaking group or enrolling in a public speaking course. These environments provide a supportive community where you can practice your speech in front of others. Feedback from fellow speakers can be invaluable in refining your delivery and boosting your confidence.

Lastly, remember that practice makes perfect. Rehearse your speech repeatedly until you feel comfortable and confident with the content and delivery. The more familiar you are with your speech, the easier it will be to adapt and respond to unexpected situations during your presentation.

In conclusion, rehearsing and practicing your speech is essential to conquer the fear of public speaking. By dedicating time to prepare, practicing in front of a mirror or a supportive audience, and seeking feedback, you will empower yourself to speak with confidence. Whether you are delivering a speech on fear or any other topic, these techniques will help you deliver a memorable and impactful presentation.

One of the most effective ways to conquer fear when giving a speech is through diligent rehearsal and practice. The old saying, "practice makes perfect," is especially true when it comes to public speaking. By taking the time to prepare and rehearse your speech, you can empower yourself to speak with confidence and overcome any fears you may have.

First and foremost, it is essential to familiarize yourself with the content of your speech. Take the time to research and gather relevant information, ensuring that you have a strong foundation to build upon. Once you have a clear understanding of the topic, outline your speech to organize your thoughts and ensure a logical flow of ideas.

With a solid outline in place, it's time to start practicing. Begin by reading through your speech several times to become comfortable with the content. As you become more familiar with the words, you can start to focus on your delivery. Pay attention to your tone, pace, and body language, making adjustments as necessary to convey your message effectively.

Next, consider recording yourself while practicing. This allows you to gain a realistic perspective on how you come across to others. Listen to the recording and observe any areas where you may need improvement. Be open to constructive criticism and use it as an opportunity to grow as a speaker.

Another valuable technique is to rehearse in front of a mirror. This allows you to not only practice your delivery but also observe your body language and facial expressions. Remember to incorporate gestures and maintain eye contact, as these nonverbal cues can greatly enhance your speech.

Additionally, consider rehearsing in front of a small audience of friends or family members. Their feedback and encouragement can help build your confidence and provide valuable insights into areas that may need improvement.

Finally, don't forget to practice managing your fear and anxiety. Incorporate relaxation techniques such as deep breathing exercises or visualization before and during your speech. Remind yourself of your strengths and the reason why you are speaking on this topic, focusing on the positive impact you can make.

In conclusion, rehearsing and practicing your speech is crucial in conquering fear and empowering yourself to speak with confidence. By familiarizing yourself with the content, refining your delivery, and managing your anxiety, you can deliver a compelling speech that leaves a lasting impact on your audience. Remember, practice makes perfect, and with dedication and perseverance, you can overcome any fear of public speaking and become a confident and powerful speaker.

Chapter 5: Handling Nervousness and Anxiety in Real-Time

Coping Strategies for Managing Anxiety

Introduction:

Anxiety is a natural response to fear and can often be overwhelming, especially when it comes to public speaking. However, it is important to remember that anxiety is not something that needs to control you. In this subchapter, we will explore effective coping strategies that can help you manage anxiety and empower yourself to speak with confidence.

1. Deep Breathing Techniques:

One of the simplest yet most effective coping strategies for managing anxiety is deep breathing. When you feel anxious, take slow, deep breaths in through your nose and out through your mouth. Focus on your breath and allow it to calm your nerves. Deep breathing not only relaxes your body but also helps to clear your mind, allowing you to focus on your speech.

2. Positive Self-Talk:

Positive self-talk plays a crucial role in managing anxiety. Instead of allowing negative thoughts to consume you, replace them with positive affirmations. Remind yourself of your strengths, capabilities, and past successes. By reinforcing positive thoughts, you can boost your confidence and reduce anxiety levels.

3. Visualization:

Visualization is a powerful technique that can help you overcome anxiety. Before your speech, close your eyes and imagine yourself delivering a successful and confident presentation. Visualize the audience responding positively and applauding your efforts. By rehearsing the scenario in your mind, you can build confidence and reduce anxiety.

4. Gradual Exposure:

Gradual exposure is a coping strategy that involves gradually exposing yourself to situations that make you anxious. Start with smaller speaking engagements, such as speaking in front of a small group of friends or colleagues. As you gain confidence, gradually increase the size of your audience. By gradually exposing yourself to anxiety-inducing situations, you can build resilience and manage your fears effectively.

5. Seek Support:

Lastly, don't hesitate to seek support from trusted friends, family, or professionals. Sharing your anxieties and fears with others can provide you with valuable insights and emotional support. Consider joining public speaking clubs or workshops where you can learn from experienced speakers and share your experiences with like-minded individuals.

Conclusion:

Managing anxiety is a crucial aspect of conquering fear and empowering yourself to speak with confidence. By incorporating these coping strategies into your routine, you can effectively manage anxiety before and during public speaking engagements. Remember, anxiety is a natural response, but it doesn't have to control you. With practice and perseverance, you can overcome your fears and deliver powerful speeches that captivate your audience.

Anxiety can be a debilitating force when it comes to public speaking. The fear of judgment, criticism, or failure can leave even the most confident individuals feeling overwhelmed with anxiety. However, it is important to remember that anxiety is a natural response to stress, and there are strategies that can help you manage and overcome it. In this subchapter, we will explore some effective coping strategies that can empower you to speak with confidence, regardless of your fear.

1. Deep Breathing: One of the simplest yet most powerful techniques for managing anxiety is deep breathing. By taking slow, deep breaths, you can activate your body's relaxation response, reducing the physical symptoms of anxiety such as rapid heartbeat and shallow breathing. Practice deep breathing exercises before and during your speech to help calm your nerves.

2. Visualization: Use the power of your imagination to visualize yourself delivering a successful speech. Close your eyes and picture yourself speaking confidently, engaging with your audience, and receiving positive feedback. Visualizing success can help shift your mindset from fear to empowerment.

3. Positive Self-Talk: Challenge negative thoughts and replace them with positive affirmations. Remind yourself that you are prepared, knowledgeable, and capable of delivering a great speech. Repeat these positive statements to yourself before and during your presentation to boost your confidence and reduce anxiety.

4. Practice and Preparation: The more prepared you are, the more confident you will feel. Practice your speech multiple times, focusing on your delivery, body language, and content. Familiarize yourself with the venue and equipment to minimize unexpected surprises. The more you practice, the more comfortable you will become, and the less anxious you will feel.

5. Progressive Muscle Relaxation: Progressive muscle relaxation is a technique that involves tensing and then releasing different muscle groups in your body. By systematically tensing and relaxing your muscles, you can release physical tension and promote relaxation. Incorporate this technique into your pre-speech routine to help manage anxiety.

6. Seek Support: Don't hesitate to reach out to friends, family, or a support group for encouragement and advice. Sharing your fears and concerns with someone can help alleviate anxiety and provide you with valuable insights and strategies.

Remember, anxiety is a normal part of the public speaking experience. By practicing these coping strategies, you can conquer your fear and empower yourself to speak with confidence.

Anxiety can be debilitating, especially when it comes to speaking in public or addressing our fears. However, with the right coping strategies, we can learn to manage and conquer our anxieties, empowering ourselves to speak with confidence. In this subchapter, we will explore various techniques to help you overcome anxiety and deliver powerful speeches on fear.

1. Deep Breathing: When anxiety strikes, our breathing becomes shallow and rapid. Practicing deep breathing exercises can help calm your nervous system, reduce anxiety, and increase focus. Take slow, deep breaths in through your nose, hold for a few seconds, and exhale slowly through your mouth. Repeat this process several times until you feel more centered and relaxed.

2. Visualization: Mental imagery is a powerful tool to combat anxiety. Visualize yourself delivering a successful speech with confidence and poise. Imagine the audience applauding and feeling inspired by your words. By repeatedly visualizing positive outcomes, you can rewire your brain to associate speaking with positive emotions, reducing anxiety in the process.

3. Positive Affirmations: Negative self-talk can fuel anxiety and hinder our ability to speak confidently. Counteract this by using positive affirmations. Repeat statements such as "I am a confident speaker," "I have valuable insights to share," and "I can overcome my fears" to boost your self-confidence and reduce anxiety.

4. Preparation and Practice: Being well-prepared is key to managing anxiety. Research your topic thoroughly, organize your thoughts, and practice your speech multiple times. The more familiar you become with your content, the more confident you will feel when delivering it.

5. Progressive Muscle Relaxation: Tension often accompanies anxiety. Progressive muscle relaxation involves tensing and then slowly releasing different muscle groups in your body to promote relaxation. Start with your toes and work your way up to your head, tensing each muscle group for a few seconds before releasing. This technique can help release physical tension and alleviate anxiety.

6. Seek Support: Don't be afraid to reach out for support. Talk to friends, family, or a therapist about your fears and anxieties. Sharing your concerns can provide emotional relief and valuable advice from others who have overcome similar challenges.

Remember, managing anxiety is a journey that requires patience and practice. By implementing these coping strategies, you can conquer your fears and empower yourself to speak with confidence.

Deep Breathing Techniques

In the journey of conquering fear and empowering yourself to speak with confidence, one powerful tool that can help you navigate through anxiety-ridden situations is deep breathing techniques. Whether you are preparing for a public speaking engagement, a job interview, or any situation that induces fear, mastering the art of deep breathing can be your secret weapon.

Deep breathing is a simple yet effective method to calm your mind, relax your body, and bring your focus to the present moment. It helps counteract the fight-or-flight response that fear triggers within us, allowing you to regain control over your emotions and thoughts. By incorporating deep breathing into your daily routine, you can build resilience and develop the ability to face your fears head-on.

There are various deep breathing techniques you can explore, each with its own benefits. One popular method is diaphragmatic breathing or belly breathing. To practice this technique, sit or lie down in a comfortable position, place one hand on your chest and the other on your abdomen. Take a slow, deep breath in through your nose, allowing your belly to rise as you fill your lungs with air. Then, exhale slowly through your mouth, feeling your belly lower. Repeat this process several times, focusing on the sensation of your breath moving in and out of your body.

Another technique that can be particularly helpful in moments of acute anxiety or panic is box breathing. This method involves inhaling, holding your breath, exhaling, and holding your breath again, each for a specific count of seconds. By practicing this pattern, you can regulate your breathing, reduce stress, and promote a sense of calmness.

In addition to these techniques, incorporating mindful breathing exercises into your daily routine can have long-lasting effects on your overall well-being. Taking a few moments each day to focus solely on your breath can help you cultivate self-awareness, improve concentration, and enhance your ability to manage fear and anxiety.

Remember, deep breathing is not a quick fix, but rather a skill that requires consistent practice to master. By incorporating these techniques into your daily life, you will gradually build a foundation of inner strength and resilience. So, take a deep breath, embrace the power of your breath, and step into the spotlight with confidence.

In the realm of public speaking, fear is a common and formidable opponent that can hinder our ability to communicate effectively. The mere thought of standing in front of a crowd can send shivers down the spine of even the most seasoned speakers. However, there are powerful techniques that can help us conquer this fear and empower ourselves to speak with confidence. One such technique is deep breathing.

Deep breathing is a simple yet incredibly effective tool that can calm our nerves, reduce anxiety, and improve our speaking performance. By taking slow, deep breaths, we can activate our body's relaxation response, which counteracts the physiological effects of fear. This technique not only helps us feel more composed but also enhances our ability to think clearly and speak fluently.

So, how can we incorporate deep breathing into our public speaking routine? One approach is to practice deep breathing exercises before stepping onto the stage. Find a quiet place where you can sit comfortably and close your eyes. Slowly inhale through your nose, allowing your abdomen to expand as you fill your lungs with air. Hold the breath for a moment, and then exhale slowly through your mouth, feeling the tension melt away with each breath. Repeat this process several times, focusing on the sensation of your breath flowing in and out.

During your speech, it's essential to continue utilizing deep breathing techniques to stay grounded and composed. Take brief pauses between sentences or thoughts to take a deep breath. This allows you to regain your composure, maintain a steady pace, and deliver your message with confidence. By consciously incorporating deep breathing into your speaking rhythm, you can harness its power to combat fear-induced symptoms like shaky voice, rapid heartbeat, and sweaty palms.

In addition to its immediate benefits, deep breathing can also have long-term effects on our overall well-being. Regular practice of deep breathing techniques can help us develop greater self-awareness and emotional resilience. As we become more attuned to our breath, we learn to manage stress and anxiety not only in public speaking scenarios but also in our daily lives.

In conclusion, deep breathing is a valuable tool in conquering the fear of public speaking and empowering ourselves to communicate confidently. By incorporating deep breathing exercises into our routine, both before and during speeches, we can cultivate a sense of calm, clarity, and control. So take a deep breath, step onto the stage, and let your words flow with confidence.

In the pursuit of conquering fear and empowering oneself to speak with confidence, it is crucial to explore various techniques that can help manage and overcome anxiety. One such technique that has proven to be effective is deep breathing. Deep breathing exercises can serve as a powerful tool to calm the mind, relax the body, and alleviate the physical symptoms of fear and anxiety.

Deep breathing involves taking slow, deliberate breaths, fully expanding the lungs and diaphragm. By focusing on the breath, we can redirect our attention away from anxious thoughts and bring ourselves into the present moment. This helps to activate the body's relaxation response, decreasing heart rate and blood pressure while increasing feelings of calmness and tranquility.

There are several deep breathing techniques that you can incorporate into your daily routine to combat fear and anxiety before delivering a speech. One popular technique is called diaphragmatic breathing, also known as belly breathing. To practice this method, find a comfortable seated position and place one hand on your chest and the other on your abdomen. Inhale deeply through your nose, allowing your abdomen to rise as you fill your lungs with air. Exhale slowly through your mouth, feeling your abdomen fall. Focus on the sensation of your breath as it enters and leaves your body, letting go of any tension or fear with each exhale.

Another effective deep breathing technique is 4-7-8 breathing. This technique involves inhaling for a count of four, holding your breath for a count of seven, and exhaling for a count of eight. This pattern helps to regulate breathing and activate the body's relaxation response.

Incorporating deep breathing into your daily routine can have numerous benefits beyond managing fear and anxiety before a speech. Regular practice of deep breathing techniques can improve overall well-being, enhance concentration, and promote better sleep. By cultivating a habit of deep breathing, you can develop a sense of inner calm and harness the power to speak with confidence in any situation.

Remember, deep breathing is a simple yet effective technique that can be practiced by anyone. Whether you are a seasoned public speaker or someone who fears speaking in front of others, incorporating deep breathing techniques into your routine can provide you with the tools to conquer fear and empower yourself to speak with confidence.

Positive Visualization during Presentations

Public speaking is a common fear that many individuals struggle with. The mere thought of standing in front of a crowd, delivering a speech, can send shivers down the spine. However, there are techniques that can help conquer this fear and empower individuals to speak with confidence. One such technique is positive visualization.

Positive visualization is a powerful tool that can be utilized to calm nerves and boost confidence during presentations. It involves creating mental images of successfully delivering a speech, envisioning a positive outcome, and feeling the surge of self-assurance that comes with it. By incorporating positive visualization into your presentation routine, you can transform your fear into excitement and conquer the stage with confidence.

To begin, find a quiet and comfortable space where you can relax and focus. Close your eyes and take deep, calming breaths. Visualize yourself standing confidently in front of the audience, feeling calm and composed. Imagine the audience responding positively to your words, nodding in agreement, and applauding your efforts. Picture yourself delivering your speech flawlessly, with a clear and confident voice. Visualize the audience engaged and captivated by your message.

As you engage in positive visualization, immerse yourself in the emotions associated with a successful presentation. Feel the excitement, joy, and pride that comes with delivering a great speech. Embrace the positive energy and let it flow through you. This exercise will not only help calm your nerves but also program your mind to expect success rather than failure.

Positive visualization can be further enhanced by incorporating affirmations and positive self-talk. Repeat positive statements to yourself such as "I am a confident and dynamic speaker," "I have valuable insights to share," or "I am well-prepared and knowledgeable." These affirmations will help boost your confidence and reinforce your belief in your abilities.

By incorporating positive visualization into your presentation preparation, you can transform your fear into a powerful tool for success. As you consistently practice positive visualization, you'll notice a shift in your mindset, from apprehension to excitement. This technique allows you to tap into your inner strength and present yourself with confidence, regardless of the size or importance of the audience.

Remember, conquering fear is a journey, and positive visualization is just one step along the way. With practice and perseverance, you can overcome your fear of public speaking and empower yourself to deliver impactful speeches that leave a lasting impression on your audience.

In the realm of public speaking, fear is a common and formidable enemy that can hinder even the most confident individuals. However, fear should not hold you back from expressing your ideas and making an impact through your presentations. One effective technique to conquer fear and boost your confidence is positive visualization.

Positive visualization involves creating mental images of success and positive outcomes. By vividly imagining yourself delivering a flawless presentation, captivating your audience, and receiving praise and admiration, you can reprogram your mind to believe in your abilities and overcome any fears or doubts. This powerful technique harnesses the power of the mind to shape your reality.

To start using positive visualization, find a quiet and comfortable space where you can relax and focus. Close your eyes and take a few deep breaths to calm your mind. Imagine yourself standing confidently on stage, feeling relaxed and in control. Visualize the audience engaged and attentive, hanging onto your every word. See yourself speaking with clarity and conviction, exuding confidence and passion. Picture the positive reactions from your audience as they nod in agreement and applaud enthusiastically at the end of your presentation.

As you continue to practice positive visualization, try to engage all your senses. Feel the warmth of the stage lights on your face, hear the supportive applause, and even imagine the smell of success in the air. The more vividly you can imagine these scenarios, the more powerful your visualization becomes.

In addition to visualizing success, it is important to accompany these mental images with positive affirmations. Repeat uplifting statements to yourself such as, "I am a confident and captivating presenter," or "My words have the power to inspire and influence others." These affirmations reinforce your belief in your abilities and help you stay focused on the positive aspects of your presentation.

Positive visualization is a valuable tool that can transform your mindset and empower you to speak with confidence. By consistently practicing this technique, you will gradually overcome your fears and anxieties associated with public speaking. Remember, fear is just an illusion that can be conquered with the power of your mind. Embrace positive visualization and watch your presentations reach new heights of success and impact.

Presenting in front of an audience can trigger a wave of fear and anxiety for many people. The fear of public speaking is one of the most common phobias, causing individuals to lose their confidence and struggle to articulate their thoughts effectively. However, with the right mindset and tools, this fear can be conquered, and you can learn to speak with confidence. One powerful technique to help you overcome your fear and deliver a successful presentation is positive visualization.

Positive visualization is a mental exercise that involves creating vivid and positive images in your mind. By visualizing yourself speaking confidently and engaging with your audience, you can rewire your brain to believe in your abilities and boost your self-confidence. This technique is backed by scientific research and has been proven to have a significant impact on performance and reducing anxiety.

To begin with, find a quiet and comfortable space where you can relax and focus. Close your eyes and take a few deep breaths to calm your mind. Visualize yourself standing on a stage, feeling calm and composed. Imagine the audience before you, eagerly listening to your every word. Picture yourself speaking with clarity, using confident body language, and making eye contact with your audience. Visualize their positive reactions, nodding heads, and warm smiles, as they are captivated by your speech.

As you continue to visualize, pay attention to the details. Imagine the sound of your voice, clear and powerful, resonating throughout the room. Feel the adrenaline coursing through your veins, energizing you and enhancing your performance. Envision yourself handling unexpected challenges or questions with ease and grace. Embrace the feeling of success and accomplishment as you receive a round of applause at the end of your presentation.

By regularly practicing positive visualization, you can reprogram your subconscious mind to believe in your ability to speak with confidence. This technique helps to reduce anxiety, boost self-esteem, and enhance your overall presentation skills. Remember, your mind is a powerful tool, and by harnessing its potential through positive visualization, you can conquer your fear of public speaking and become a captivating and confident presenter.

In conclusion, positive visualization is a valuable technique that can empower you to overcome your fear of public speaking and deliver compelling presentations. By visualizing yourself speaking confidently and engaging with your audience, you can rewire your brain to believe in your abilities and boost your self-confidence. Incorporate this practice into your preparation routine and watch as it transforms your mindset and performance on stage. Embrace the power of positive visualization, conquer your fear, and become a confident speaker who captivates their audience.

Mindfulness Practices for Calming Nerves

In our quest to conquer fear and speak with confidence, it is essential to cultivate a sense of calmness and control over our nerves. One powerful tool that can aid us in this journey is the practice of mindfulness. Mindfulness allows us to be fully present in the moment, observing our thoughts and emotions without judgment. By incorporating mindfulness practices into our daily lives, we can develop a greater sense of self-awareness, enhance our ability to stay centered, and ultimately overcome our fear of speaking.

One effective mindfulness practice for calming nerves is deep breathing. When we feel anxious or nervous, our breath tends to become shallow and rapid. By consciously slowing down and deepening our breaths, we can activate the body's relaxation response. Take a moment to close your eyes, inhale deeply through your nose, hold it for a few seconds, and then exhale slowly through your mouth. Repeat this process several times, allowing yourself to fully relax with each breath.

Another valuable mindfulness technique is body scanning. Close your eyes and bring your attention to your body. Start from the top of your head and slowly move down, paying attention to any areas of tension or discomfort. As you identify these areas, consciously relax them, releasing any built-up stress. By systematically scanning your body, you can release physical tension and create a sense of ease and relaxation.

Additionally, incorporating a daily meditation practice can significantly reduce anxiety and nervousness. Find a quiet and comfortable space, sit in a relaxed position, and focus on your breath or a specific mantra. As thoughts arise, acknowledge them without judgment and gently bring your attention back to your breath or mantra. Consistent meditation practice can train your mind to stay focused and calm, even in high-pressure situations like public speaking.

Lastly, practicing gratitude can help shift your mindset from fear to positivity. Take a few moments each day to reflect on the things you are grateful for. By acknowledging the positive aspects of your life, you cultivate a sense of abundance and contentment, reducing feelings of anxiety and fear.

In conclusion, incorporating mindfulness practices into your daily routine can be immensely beneficial in conquering the fear of speaking. By engaging in deep breathing, body scanning, meditation, and gratitude exercises, you can cultivate a sense of calmness, enhance self-awareness, and empower yourself to speak with confidence. Remember, mindfulness is a lifelong practice, and with consistent effort, you can transform your relationship with fear and step into your true potential as a speaker.

Introduction:
In our fast-paced and demanding world, it is common for many of us to experience nervousness and anxiety when it comes to public speaking or addressing our fears. The good news is that mindfulness practices can help us conquer these fears and empower ourselves to speak with confidence. By incorporating simple techniques into our daily lives, we can calm our nerves and enhance our ability to communicate effectively. In this subchapter, we will explore several

mindfulness practices specifically designed to alleviate anxiety and promote a sense of calm when speaking about our fears.

1.   Deep   Breathing:
One of the most effective ways to calm nerves is to focus on deep, slow breathing. By taking deep breaths, we activate the body's relaxation response, which helps to reduce stress and anxiety. Practice inhaling deeply through your nose, holding the breath for a few seconds, and then exhaling slowly through your mouth. Repeat this process several times before and during a speech or discussion to bring about a sense of calm and centeredness.

2.   Grounding   Techniques:
Another powerful practice is grounding oneself in the present moment. When nerves kick in, we tend to get lost in our thoughts and worries, which can distract us from the task at hand. To counteract this, try grounding techniques such as focusing on the sensation of your feet on the ground or the feeling of your breath moving in and out of your body. This helps to anchor your attention in the present moment, allowing you to speak with more clarity and confidence.

3.   Visualization:
Visualization is a powerful tool for calming nerves and boosting confidence. Before a speech or discussion, spend a few moments visualizing yourself delivering your message with ease and grace. Imagine the positive reactions from the audience and the sense of accomplishment that follows. By mentally rehearsing success, you will build confidence and reduce anxiety.

4.   Mindful   Self-Compassion:

When fear arises, it is important to be kind and compassionate to ourselves. Practice self-compassion by acknowledging and accepting your nervousness without judgment. Remind yourself that it is natural to feel anxious and that you are capable of managing it. Treat yourself with kindness and understanding, just as you would a close friend.

Conclusion:

Mindfulness practices offer a powerful toolkit for calming nerves and empowering yourself to speak with confidence. By incorporating deep breathing, grounding techniques, visualization, and mindful self-compassion into your daily routine, you will develop the skills necessary to conquer your fears and effectively communicate your message. Remember, everyone experiences nervousness at some point, but with practice and mindfulness, you can overcome it and become a confident speaker.

Introduction:

In our journey to conquer fear and become confident speakers, it is essential to address the nerves that often accompany public speaking. Fear can manifest in various ways, such as a racing heart, sweaty palms, or a shaky voice. These physical symptoms can hinder our ability to communicate effectively. However, through the practice of mindfulness, we can learn to calm our nerves and reclaim our confidence. This subchapter explores mindfulness practices specifically tailored to address nerves when delivering speeches on fear.

1.   Breathing   Techniques:

One of the most effective ways to calm nerves is through conscious breathing. By focusing on our breath, we ground ourselves in the present moment, reducing anxiety and promoting relaxation. Try deep belly breathing, inhaling slowly through the nose, feeling the breath fill your abdomen, and exhaling gently through the mouth. This technique slows down the heart rate and provides a sense of calm.

2. Body Scan Meditation: Before delivering a speech, take a moment to connect with your body through a body scan meditation. Start from the top of your head and slowly move down, observing any tension or discomfort. Allow your breath to flow through those areas, helping to release any physical or mental tension. This practice promotes self-awareness and helps calm nerves by acknowledging and releasing any bodily stress.

3. Visualization: Visualization is a powerful tool for calming nerves. Close your eyes and visualize yourself delivering a successful speech with confidence and grace. Imagine the positive reactions from the audience and the feeling of accomplishment. By repeatedly visualizing success, you rewire your brain to associate public speaking with positive emotions, reducing fear and anxiety.

4. Grounding Techniques: When nerves strike, it can be helpful to ground yourself in the present moment. Engage your senses by focusing on what you see, hear, smell, taste, and touch. Feel the floor beneath your feet, listen to the sounds around you, or observe a specific object. This practice redirects your attention away from anxiety-inducing thoughts and brings you back to the present, where you can regain control.

Conclusion:

Mindfulness practices offer invaluable techniques to calm nerves and empower ourselves to speak with confidence. By incorporating breathing techniques, body scan meditations, visualization, and grounding techniques into our routine, we can effectively manage the anxiety that often accompanies speech on fear. Remember, conquering fear is a journey, and with consistent mindfulness practice, we can transform nervousness into empowerment and become confident speakers who captivate and inspire our audience.

Utilizing Audience Engagement to Alleviate Fear

Fear is a powerful emotion that can often cripple us, especially when it comes to public speaking. The mere thought of standing in front of a crowd can evoke anxiety and self-doubt. However, there is a powerful tool that can help alleviate this fear: audience engagement.

Engaging your audience is not only a way to captivate their attention, but it also provides a means to conquer your own fears. By involving your listeners in your speech on fear, you not only create a more interactive experience, but you also shift the focus away from your own anxieties. Here, we will explore the various techniques and strategies to effectively utilize audience engagement to alleviate fear and empower yourself to speak with confidence.

One of the most effective ways to engage your audience is through interactive exercises. These exercises can range from simple icebreakers to more elaborate group activities. By actively involving your listeners, you create a sense of shared experience, making them feel more connected to your message. This connection helps to ease your own fear, as you are no longer speaking to a faceless crowd but rather a group of individuals with whom you have formed a bond.

Another powerful tool for audience engagement is storytelling. Sharing personal anecdotes or relatable stories not only captivates your listeners but also humanizes you as a speaker. When your audience sees you as a relatable individual who has experienced fear, just like them, it creates a sense of empathy and understanding. This empathy helps to alleviate fear, as you realize that you are not alone in your anxieties.

Additionally, incorporating visual aids and multimedia can enhance audience engagement. Technology offers a wide range of options, from slideshows to videos, that can help illustrate your points and create a more dynamic presentation. These visual aids not only capture attention but also provide a distraction from your own fears, allowing you to focus on delivering your message with confidence.

In conclusion, audience engagement is a powerful tool that can alleviate fear and empower you to speak with confidence. By actively involving your listeners through interactive exercises, storytelling, and visual aids, you create a sense of connection and shared experience. As you shift the focus away from your own anxieties and make your speech on fear a collaborative effort, you will find yourself growing more confident and empowered. So, embrace the power of audience engagement and conquer your fears today!

When it comes to conquering fear and speaking with confidence, one powerful tool in your arsenal is audience engagement. Fear often stems from the unknown and the feeling of being judged. By actively involving your audience in your speech on fear, you can alleviate these fears and create a supportive and interactive environment.

One effective way to engage your audience is by starting your speech with a thought-provoking question or a relatable story. This instantly grabs their attention and makes them feel involved from the beginning. It also helps to establish a connection between you and your audience, making them more receptive to your message.

Another technique to encourage audience engagement is by incorporating interactive activities or group discussions into your speech. This not only keeps your audience actively engaged but also allows them to share their thoughts and experiences related to fear. By creating a safe space for open discussion, you provide an opportunity for individuals to confront their fears collectively, which can be incredibly empowering.

Additionally, incorporating multimedia elements such as visuals, videos, or even live demonstrations can enhance audience engagement. These visual aids not only help illustrate your points but also stimulate different senses, making your speech more memorable and impactful. Utilizing technology effectively can also help create a dynamic and engaging atmosphere during your speech.

Furthermore, don't underestimate the power of humor. Injecting appropriate humor into your speech can help lighten the mood, reduce tension, and create a relaxed atmosphere. Laughter is contagious, and when your audience is laughing and enjoying themselves, their fears automatically diminish.

Lastly, actively seeking feedback and addressing questions throughout your speech helps keep your audience engaged and ensures that their concerns are being heard. This two-way interaction fosters a sense of trust and builds a supportive environment where individuals feel comfortable sharing their fears and seeking guidance.

In conclusion, audience engagement is a powerful tool that can help alleviate fear and empower you to speak with confidence. By actively involving your audience through thought-provoking questions, interactive activities, multimedia elements, humor, and open discussions, you create a safe and supportive environment where fears can be confronted and conquered collectively. Remember, engaging with your audience is not only beneficial for them but also for your own growth as a speaker.

When it comes to delivering a speech on fear, one of the most effective techniques to empower yourself and connect with your audience is by utilizing audience engagement strategies. Engaging your audience not only helps to alleviate your own fear but also creates a supportive and interactive environment that fosters a sense of connection and understanding.

To begin with, incorporating audience participation can help to break the ice and create a relaxed atmosphere. By encouraging your audience to share their own experiences and thoughts related to fear, you can establish a common ground and demonstrate that fear is a universal emotion that everyone experiences at some point in their lives. This shared understanding helps to alleviate the pressure and fear of being judged, allowing you to feel more confident and at ease.

Furthermore, involving your audience in activities or exercises related to fear can be an effective way to keep their attention and create a dynamic presentation. For instance, you can ask them to participate in a brief role-playing exercise where they have to confront a fear or share strategies they have used to overcome fear in the past. This not only makes your speech more interactive but also provides valuable insights and perspectives that can enhance the overall message of your talk.

Another technique to engage your audience is by using storytelling. Narrating personal experiences or sharing anecdotes of individuals who have successfully conquered their fears can be incredibly inspiring and relatable. By weaving these stories into your speech, you can captivate your audience's attention and create an emotional connection. This emotional connection not only makes your speech more memorable but also helps to alleviate fear by showing that others have faced similar challenges and come out victorious.

In addition to these strategies, utilizing visual aids such as videos, images, or props can also enhance audience engagement. Visuals have the power to evoke emotions and create a deeper impact on your audience. They can serve as powerful tools to illustrate concepts, provide examples, or even share quotes that resonate with the theme of conquering fear.

Overall, audience engagement is a powerful tool to alleviate fear and empower yourself when delivering a speech on the topic. By incorporating interactive exercises, storytelling, and visual aids, you can create a supportive and engaging environment that connects with your audience on a deeper level. Remember, fear is a universal emotion, and by sharing your own vulnerabilities and experiences, you can inspire others to conquer their own fears and speak with confidence.

Establishing Rapport with the Audience

When it comes to delivering a speech on fear, one of the most crucial aspects is establishing rapport with your audience. Rapport is the foundation upon which a successful speech is built, as it allows you to connect with your listeners on a deeper level and gain their trust and attention. In this subchapter, we will explore various techniques and strategies that will empower you to establish rapport with any audience, regardless of their size or background.

First and foremost, it is important to acknowledge that fear is a universal emotion. Every individual in your audience has experienced fear at some point in their lives, whether it be the fear of failure, rejection, or the unknown. By recognizing and empathizing with this shared experience, you can create an immediate bond with your listeners. Begin your speech by sharing a personal anecdote or story that highlights your own struggles with fear. This vulnerability will not only humanize you but also make your audience feel understood and connected.

Another effective technique for establishing rapport is active listening. As you deliver your speech, pay attention to the nonverbal cues and reactions of your audience. Maintain eye contact and be responsive to their body language. If you notice signs of confusion or disinterest, adjust your delivery accordingly. Engaging your audience in this way demonstrates that you value their presence and opinions, fostering a sense of mutual respect and understanding.

In addition to active listening, it is crucial to tailor your speech to the specific needs and interests of your audience. Before your presentation, take the time to research and understand the demographics, backgrounds, and concerns of those you will be addressing. This will allow you to craft your speech in a way that resonates with their unique experiences and challenges. By addressing their specific fears and offering practical solutions, you will establish yourself as a credible and relatable speaker.

Lastly, don't underestimate the power of humor. Fear can be an overwhelming and serious topic, but injecting moments of levity into your speech can help alleviate tension and create a more relaxed atmosphere. By sharing lighthearted anecdotes or incorporating witty remarks, you can engage your audience and make them feel more comfortable. Laughter is a powerful tool for building rapport and fostering a positive connection with your listeners.

In conclusion, establishing rapport with your audience is essential when delivering a speech on fear. By acknowledging their shared experiences, actively listening, tailoring your speech to their needs, and incorporating humor, you can create a strong bond and gain their trust and attention. Remember, your audience is there to learn from you and be inspired. By establishing rapport, you empower yourself to speak with confidence and make a lasting impact on those who listen to your message.

When it comes to delivering a speech on fear, one of the most critical factors for success lies in establishing a strong rapport with your audience. The ability to connect with your listeners on a personal level not only helps to capture their attention but also creates a safe and comfortable environment for them to engage with your message. In this subchapter, we will explore effective techniques to establish rapport with your audience, empowering you to speak with confidence and inspire others to conquer their fears.

First and foremost, it's essential to acknowledge and understand the fears your audience may have. By recognizing their concerns, you demonstrate empathy and show that you are genuinely interested in their well-being. This can be achieved by conducting thorough research, engaging in conversations, and actively listening to their stories and experiences. By doing so, you will be able to tailor your speech to address their specific fears and aspirations, making it more relatable and impactful.

Another powerful way to establish rapport is through storytelling. Sharing personal anecdotes or real-life examples not only humanizes you as a speaker but also helps your audience connect with your message on an emotional level. By recounting your own journey of conquering fear, you demonstrate that you understand their struggles and provide them with a roadmap for overcoming their own fears. Utilize vivid descriptions, humor, and emotions to captivate your audience and keep them engaged throughout your speech.

Furthermore, body language plays a crucial role in establishing rapport. Maintain eye contact with your audience, as it conveys trust and confidence. Use open and welcoming gestures to create a warm and inclusive atmosphere. Pay attention to your facial expressions, ensuring they reflect genuine enthusiasm and sincerity. Non-verbal cues can significantly impact the audience's perception of you and your message, so being mindful of your body language is essential.

Lastly, encourage audience participation and interaction. Incorporate activities, such as group discussions or Q&A sessions, to actively involve your listeners. This not only helps to break the ice but also fosters a sense of community and collaboration. By creating an inclusive environment where everyone feels comfortable sharing their thoughts and fears, you empower them to overcome their anxieties and take an active role in their personal growth.

In conclusion, establishing rapport with your audience is a fundamental aspect of delivering a powerful speech on fear. By acknowledging their fears, sharing personal stories, utilizing effective body language, and encouraging audience participation, you can create a safe and engaging environment that empowers individuals to conquer their fears. Remember, the key lies in connecting with your audience on a personal level, demonstrating empathy, and inspiring them to take action towards a fear-free life.

When it comes to speaking in public, one of the most crucial factors in ensuring a successful delivery is establishing a strong rapport with your audience. Building a connection with those who are listening to your speech on fear can make all the difference in capturing their attention, keeping them engaged, and ultimately conveying your message effectively. In this subchapter, we will explore some valuable strategies to help you establish rapport and empower yourself to speak with confidence.

First and foremost, it is important to recognize that your audience is made up of individuals who are seeking information, inspiration, or a solution to a problem. By acknowledging this and demonstrating empathy, you can create an immediate bond. Begin by sharing personal anecdotes or experiences related to fear that your audience can relate to. This vulnerability will not only make you more relatable, but it will also create a safe and comfortable environment for your listeners to engage with you.

Another effective way to establish rapport is through the use of language and tone. Tailor your speech to the knowledge level and interests of the audience. Avoid using jargon or technical terms that may alienate those who are unfamiliar with the subject matter. Instead, opt for clear, concise, and accessible language that ensures everyone can understand and connect with your message.

Non-verbal communication also plays a significant role in rapport-building. Maintain eye contact with your audience, use friendly gestures, and project a confident posture. These actions will convey your sincerity and interest in connecting with them on a personal level.

Additionally, actively involving your audience in your speech can foster a sense of belonging and engagement. Ask thought-provoking questions, encourage participation, and create opportunities for them to share their own experiences or fears. This interactive approach will not only make your speech more dynamic but will also leave a lasting impression on your audience.

Lastly, remember the power of storytelling. Humans are wired to respond to narratives, so weave compelling stories into your speech on fear. By sharing stories that resonate with your audience, you will be able to captivate their attention and create an emotional connection that inspires and motivates them.

In conclusion, establishing rapport with your audience is a vital step in conquering your fear of public speaking. By employing these strategies - sharing personal experiences, using accessible language, utilizing non-verbal communication, encouraging audience participation, and incorporating storytelling - you can empower yourself to speak with confidence and leave a lasting impact on every individual in the room.

Incorporating Interactive Elements in Your Speech

When it comes to public speaking, one of the most effective ways to engage your audience and conquer fear is by incorporating interactive elements into your speech. By involving your audience in the conversation, you not only captivate their attention but also create a memorable experience that leaves a lasting impact. In this subchapter, we will explore various interactive techniques that you can incorporate into your speech on fear, allowing you to empower yourself and speak with confidence.

One powerful interactive element is the use of rhetorical questions. By posing thought-provoking questions to your audience, you encourage them to reflect on their own fears and experiences. This not only stimulates their thinking but also creates a sense of involvement and participation. For example, you might ask, "Have you ever felt paralyzed by fear? What strategies have you used to overcome it?" By inviting your audience to share their thoughts, you create a safe and inclusive environment for discussion.

Another interactive technique is storytelling. Humans have an innate affinity for stories, and by weaving personal anecdotes or relatable narratives into your speech, you can connect with your audience on a deeper level. Share your own experiences of overcoming fear, and encourage your listeners to share theirs. This not only fosters a sense of camaraderie but also provides valuable insights and inspiration for others facing similar challenges.

In addition to rhetorical questions and storytelling, incorporating interactive exercises can heighten audience engagement even further.

Consider incorporating small group discussions, role-playing scenarios, or interactive polls to encourage active participation. These activities allow your audience to apply the concepts you discuss in real-time, fostering a deeper understanding and personal connection to the topic of fear.

Remember that incorporating interactive elements in your speech requires careful planning and consideration. Be mindful of the time constraints and adapt the activities to suit the size and dynamics of your audience. Keep the atmosphere light, supportive, and non-judgmental, allowing everyone to feel comfortable sharing their thoughts and experiences.

By incorporating interactive elements into your speech on fear, you transform a traditional lecture into an engaging and empowering experience. Your audience will not only learn from your expertise but also from each other, creating a collaborative environment where fears are confronted and conquered together. So, go ahead and embrace the power of interaction in your speeches to conquer fear and empower yourself and others to speak with confidence.

When it comes to public speaking, incorporating interactive elements into your speech can be a powerful tool to engage your audience and make a lasting impact. Interactive elements not only capture the attention of your listeners but also provide them with a unique and memorable experience. In this subchapter, we will explore various techniques and strategies to incorporate interactive elements into your speech, empowering you to overcome fear and speak with confidence.

One effective way to engage your audience is through the use of open-ended questions. By asking thought-provoking questions, you encourage active participation and invite your listeners to reflect on the topic at hand. This not only creates an interactive environment but also allows you to gauge the understanding and interest level of your audience.

Another interactive element you can incorporate is storytelling. Sharing personal anecdotes or relevant stories can captivate your audience's attention and make your speech more relatable. By sharing your experiences with fear and how you overcame it, you not only inspire your listeners but also create a connection with them.

Additionally, incorporating multimedia elements such as videos, images, or props can greatly enhance the interactive nature of your speech. Visual aids can help illustrate complex concepts or evoke emotions, making your message more impactful. Props, on the other hand, can create a tactile experience for your audience, allowing them to physically engage with your speech.

Furthermore, interactive exercises or activities can be incorporated to create a hands-on learning experience. For instance, you can divide your audience into small groups and assign them a task related to overcoming fear. This not only encourages collaboration but also provides an opportunity for participants to share their insights and learn from one another.

Lastly, incorporating technology can also add an interactive element to your speech. Utilizing platforms like live polls or interactive apps can enable real-time engagement and feedback from your audience. This not only keeps them actively involved but also allows you to adapt your speech based on their responses.

Incorporating interactive elements in your speech is not only beneficial for your audience but also for your own confidence. It fosters a sense of connection, creates a dynamic environment, and ensures that your message is effectively conveyed. So, embrace these techniques, conquer your fear, and empower yourself to speak with confidence. Remember, the more interactive your speech, the more memorable and impactful it will be.

Speaking in public can be a nerve-wracking experience, especially when you are addressing a topic as personal and sensitive as fear. However, incorporating interactive elements into your speech can be a powerful tool to engage your audience and make your message resonate with them on a deeper level. By fostering a sense of connection and participation, you can empower yourself to speak with confidence and effectively conquer your fear.

One effective way to incorporate interactive elements in your speech on fear is by sharing personal anecdotes and inviting your audience to do the same. Begin by recounting a personal experience where you faced and overcame your fear. This vulnerability will encourage your listeners to open up and share their own stories, creating a supportive and interactive atmosphere. By doing so, you not only validate their experiences but also establish a sense of camaraderie, showing them that they are not alone in their fears.

Another interactive element to consider is the use of visual aids. Incorporate relevant images, videos, or even props that can help illustrate your point and grab your audience's attention. For instance, if you are speaking about fear of public speaking, you could display a picture of a person confidently addressing a large audience. This visual representation can help your audience visualize success and inspire them to overcome their own fears.

Furthermore, incorporating interactive exercises or activities can enhance the impact of your speech. For example, you could ask your audience to participate in a brief mindfulness exercise, guiding them through deep breathing or visualization techniques to help calm their nerves. This not only engages your listeners actively but also provides them with practical tools to manage their fear.

Additionally, consider incorporating technology into your speech. Utilize polling apps or interactive slideshows that allow your audience to participate and provide real-time feedback. This dynamic approach not only captures their attention but also helps you gauge their understanding and adjust your speech accordingly.

Incorporating interactive elements in your speech on fear has the potential to transform it into a transformative experience for both you and your audience. By creating a safe and engaging environment, you can empower yourself and those around you to conquer their fears and speak with confidence. Remember, the power lies within you – embrace it, connect with your audience, and embark on your journey towards fearlessness.

Embracing Feedback and Constructive Criticism

In the journey of conquering fear and empowering yourself to speak with confidence, one of the most valuable tools at your disposal is feedback. Feedback, whether in the form of constructive criticism or positive reinforcement, is an essential component of personal growth and improvement. It allows you to gain insights into your strengths and weaknesses, identify areas for improvement, and ultimately become a more effective speaker.

Feedback is not always easy to receive, especially when it involves criticism. However, by embracing feedback and viewing it as an opportunity for growth, you can transform it into a powerful catalyst for improvement. Remember that feedback is not a reflection of your worth as a speaker or an individual but rather an objective assessment of your performance. It offers a fresh perspective, highlighting areas that may have gone unnoticed and providing valuable suggestions for improvement.

When receiving feedback, it is crucial to cultivate an open and receptive mindset. Instead of becoming defensive or dismissing criticism, actively listen and seek to understand the perspectives of others. Take a step back and view feedback as a valuable gift that can help you refine your skills and overcome the fear of public speaking.

Constructive criticism, in particular, is a powerful tool for growth. It provides specific suggestions and recommendations for improvement. Embrace it with gratitude and use it as a roadmap to enhance your speaking abilities. Remember, constructive criticism is not an attack on your character or abilities but an opportunity to learn and develop.

To effectively embrace feedback and constructive criticism, it is essential to create a supportive and safe environment for its exchange. Surround yourself with individuals who genuinely want to see you succeed and are willing to provide honest and helpful feedback. Seek out mentors, coaches, or fellow speakers who can offer valuable insights and guidance. Share your fears and concerns with them, and encourage them to provide honest feedback that will help you grow.

Lastly, remember that feedback is a two-way street. Just as you receive feedback, be open to providing it to others. Offer constructive criticism in a respectful and supportive manner, focusing on the person's strengths and providing suggestions for improvement. By contributing to the growth and development of others, you cultivate a culture of learning and collaboration, where everyone can thrive.

In conclusion, embracing feedback and constructive criticism is a crucial step in conquering fear and empowering yourself to speak with confidence. By adopting an open mindset, seeking out feedback, and using it as a tool for growth, you can overcome your fear of public speaking and become a more effective and influential communicator. Embrace feedback, value constructive criticism, and watch as your speaking skills soar to new heights.

In our journey to conquer fear and empower ourselves to speak with confidence, it is crucial to understand the value of feedback and constructive criticism. Whether we are delivering a speech on fear or any other topic, feedback can be the key to our growth and improvement as speakers. By embracing feedback, we open ourselves up to new perspectives, identify areas for improvement, and ultimately enhance our ability to communicate effectively.

Feedback is not always easy to receive, as it often highlights our weaknesses or areas in need of development. However, by shifting our mindset and viewing feedback as an opportunity for growth, we can leverage it to our advantage. Constructive criticism, when delivered with good intentions, can provide us with insights that we may have overlooked or been unaware of. It allows us to see our blind spots and make necessary adjustments to our speaking style, content, or delivery techniques.

One way to embrace feedback is by actively seeking it out. After delivering a speech on fear, approach trusted individuals in your audience and ask for their honest opinions. Encourage them to provide specific suggestions for improvement and welcome their insights with an open mind. Remember, feedback is not meant to tear you down, but rather to build you up and help you become a more confident speaker.

Additionally, it is essential to differentiate between constructive criticism and personal attacks. Not all feedback will be helpful or constructive, and it is crucial to filter out the negativity. Focus on the feedback that offers practical advice and actionable steps for improvement. Consider the source of the feedback as well; someone with expertise or experience in public speaking will likely provide more valuable insights than someone who simply wants to criticize.

Furthermore, self-reflection plays a significant role in embracing feedback. Take the time to evaluate your own performance objectively after delivering a speech on fear. Be honest with yourself, identify areas where you could have done better, and set goals for improvement. By taking ownership of your growth, you will be more open to feedback and motivated to implement necessary changes.

In conclusion, embracing feedback and constructive criticism is vital for anyone seeking to conquer fear and speak with confidence, especially when delivering a speech on fear. By actively seeking feedback, differentiating between constructive criticism and personal attacks, and engaging in self-reflection, we can transform feedback into a powerful tool for personal and professional growth. Let us remember that feedback is not a reflection of our worth but an opportunity to become better versions of ourselves.

Receiving feedback and constructive criticism can be a daunting task, especially when it comes to something as personal as speaking with confidence about our fears. However, learning to embrace feedback and view it as an opportunity for growth is crucial in conquering fear and empowering ourselves to speak confidently. In this subchapter, we will explore the importance of feedback, how to accept criticism gracefully, and how to use it to improve your speech on fear.

Feedback is a powerful tool that helps us gain a fresh perspective and identify areas for improvement. It allows us to see our blind spots and understand how our words and delivery impact others. By seeking feedback from a variety of sources, such as friends, family, mentors, or even audience members, we open ourselves up to valuable insights that can help us refine our message and delivery.

When receiving feedback, it is essential to cultivate a mindset of openness and receptivity. Rather than being defensive or dismissive, try to listen actively and genuinely consider the feedback you receive.

Remember that constructive criticism is not an attack on your character; it is an opportunity for growth. Embrace it as a gift that can propel you forward in your journey of conquering fear and speaking confidently.

To accept criticism gracefully, practice active listening. Be present in the moment and give your full attention to the person providing feedback. Avoid interrupting or becoming defensive. Instead, ask clarifying questions to gain a deeper understanding of their perspective. Express gratitude for their input, as it shows respect for their time and effort in helping you improve.

Once you have received feedback, it is important to reflect upon it and identify actionable steps for improvement. Look for patterns or recurring themes in the feedback you receive. Is there a particular aspect of your speech on fear that needs more attention? Are there specific areas where you can enhance your delivery or engage your audience more effectively? Use this feedback as a roadmap to refine your speaking skills and conquer your fears.

Remember, feedback is not meant to discourage or demotivate you. It is a powerful tool that, when embraced with an open mind, can help you grow and become a more confident speaker. By actively seeking feedback, accepting criticism gracefully, and using it to improve your speech on fear, you will embark on a transformative journey towards conquering your fears and empowering yourself to speak with confidence.

Chapter 6: Building Confidence through Experience

Starting Small: Practicing in Low-Stakes Environments

In the journey of conquering fear and empowering yourself to speak with confidence, starting small is a crucial step. Just like any skill, public speaking requires practice and gradual exposure to higher-stakes situations. This subchapter discusses the importance of practicing in low-stakes environments as a means to overcome the fear of public speaking.

For everyone, speaking in front of others can be intimidating, and fear often holds us back from expressing ourselves effectively. However, by starting small, we can gradually build up our confidence and master the art of public speaking.

Low-stakes environments refer to situations where the consequences of making mistakes or faltering in speech are minimal. These can include speaking in front of close friends or family, participating in small group discussions, or even recording yourself speaking alone. By practicing in these environments, you can develop your skills without the pressure of judgment or criticism.

One of the key benefits of practicing in low-stakes environments is the opportunity to experiment and refine your speaking style. You can try different techniques, gestures, or tones of voice without the fear of making a major blunder. This experimentation helps you find your unique style and build the foundation for confident public speaking.

Another advantage of starting small is that it allows you to gradually increase the difficulty level. Once you feel comfortable speaking in front of a small group, you can slowly transition to larger audiences or more formal settings. This incremental approach enables you to overcome anxiety step-by-step, building resilience and gaining experience along the way.

Furthermore, practicing in low-stakes environments helps you identify and address your specific fears and weaknesses. By analyzing your performance and seeking feedback from supportive individuals, you can develop strategies to improve and overcome any challenges you may face. This self-reflection and growth mindset are essential for continuous improvement as a speaker.

Remember, conquering fear is a process, and it takes time. Starting small and practicing in low-stakes environments is a powerful strategy to build confidence and overcome the fear of public speaking. Embrace these opportunities, experiment with different techniques, and gradually challenge yourself to speak in higher-stakes situations. With perseverance and dedication, you will transform your fear into a powerful tool for self-expression, ultimately empowering yourself to speak with confidence in any setting.

In the journey of conquering fear and empowering yourself to speak with confidence, it is crucial to start small. Just like a seed needs nurturing before it can grow into a mighty tree, your confidence in public speaking requires practice in low-stakes environments. This subchapter aims to shed light on the significance of beginning your speaking journey in safe spaces and provides practical tips to help you build a strong foundation.

Why start small? The answer lies in the nature of fear itself. Fear often arises from the unknown, the anticipation of failure, or the fear of judgment. By gradually exposing yourself to speaking opportunities in low-stakes environments, you can desensitize yourself to these fears. This approach allows you to build confidence and develop essential skills before tackling more challenging speaking engagements.

One effective strategy to start small is by engaging in conversations with friends and family. These interactions provide a comfortable setting where you can practice articulating your thoughts and ideas. Additionally, consider joining small discussion groups or clubs where you can share your opinions and insights in a supportive environment. Such platforms offer valuable opportunities to refine your speaking skills and receive constructive feedback.

Another way to practice in low-stakes environments is by utilizing virtual platforms. Online communities, webinars, or public speaking forums provide a safe space to express your thoughts and receive feedback from like-minded individuals. These platforms not only allow you to practice your speaking abilities but also help you connect with others who share similar fears and aspirations.

Furthermore, exploring hobbies or interests that involve public speaking can be an excellent way to gain experience in a low-pressure environment. Joining a local theater group, participating in storytelling events, or volunteering to lead presentations can help you gradually build confidence and overcome the fear of speaking in front of an audience.

Remember, the key to starting small is to focus on the process rather than the outcome. Embrace each opportunity as a chance to learn and grow, regardless of the outcome. By doing so, you will gradually strengthen your speaking skills, boost your confidence, and overcome fear.

In conclusion, starting small is a pivotal step in conquering fear and empowering yourself to speak with confidence. Whether it is engaging in conversations with loved ones, participating in online communities, or exploring speaking opportunities in hobbies, low-stakes environments provide the ideal setting to hone your skills. Embrace these opportunities, learn from each experience, and watch as your confidence blossoms, helping you reach new heights in your speaking journey.

Gradually Increasing the Difficulty Level of Speaking Engagements

One of the most effective strategies for conquering fear and building confidence in public speaking is to gradually increase the difficulty level of your speaking engagements. By challenging yourself to step outside of your comfort zone and tackle more demanding speaking opportunities, you can develop the skills and mindset needed to overcome your fear and speak with confidence.

When it comes to public speaking, fear is often rooted in the unknown. We fear the judgment of others, making mistakes, or forgetting our lines. However, the more we expose ourselves to different speaking situations, the more familiar and comfortable we become. This is where gradually increasing the difficulty level of speaking engagements comes into play.

Start by identifying your comfort zone. What types of speaking engagements do you feel relatively at ease with? Perhaps it's speaking in small groups or delivering presentations to colleagues. Once you have identified your comfort zone, it's time to step slightly outside of it. Look for opportunities that push your boundaries just a little, without overwhelming you.

For example, if you are comfortable speaking in front of small groups, consider volunteering to present to a larger audience. This could be at a local community event or a company-wide meeting. By gradually increasing the size of your audience, you expose yourself to new challenges while still maintaining a level of familiarity.

Another way to increase the difficulty level is to diversify the topics you speak about. If you tend to stick to subjects you are knowledgeable and comfortable with, try branching out into new areas. This forces you to research and prepare for unfamiliar topics, enhancing your ability to adapt and think on your feet.

As you continue to push yourself out of your comfort zone, you will notice that your fear diminishes and your confidence grows. You become more resilient and better equipped to handle unexpected situations. Remember, the goal is not to jump from your comfort zone to the most challenging speaking engagements overnight. Gradual progression is key to building confidence and conquering fear.

In conclusion, gradually increasing the difficulty level of speaking engagements is a powerful strategy for overcoming fear and speaking with confidence. By stepping outside of your comfort zone, whether it's by speaking to larger audiences or tackling unfamiliar topics, you expose yourself to new challenges that ultimately make you a stronger and more confident speaker. Embrace these opportunities, grow from them, and watch your fear transform into empowerment.

In the journey of conquering fear and empowering yourself to speak with confidence, it is essential to gradually increase the difficulty level of your speaking engagements. This subchapter will guide you through the importance of this progression and provide practical tips to help you succeed in delivering impactful speeches on fear.

When it comes to public speaking, stepping out of your comfort zone is crucial for personal growth. By gradually increasing the difficulty level of your speaking engagements, you challenge yourself to overcome different obstacles, expand your limits, and develop a strong foundation of confidence. This progression allows you to tackle more complex topics related to fear, enabling you to become a voice of inspiration and empowerment.

To begin, start with smaller speaking engagements, such as speaking in front of friends, family, or a small group of supportive individuals. This will help you build your confidence and gain valuable experience in controlling your nerves. Once you feel comfortable in these settings, gradually move on to larger audiences, such as speaking at local community events or workshops. This progression will help you adapt to various environments and gain exposure to different challenges.

As you increase the difficulty level, consider exploring niche areas of speech on fear. Dive into specific aspects of fear that resonate with you, such as overcoming personal fears, managing fear in the workplace, or techniques for fear reduction. By focusing on these niches, you can deliver more impactful speeches that connect with your audience on a deeper level, as they can relate to your personal experiences and insights.

To succeed in gradually increasing the difficulty level, it is crucial to practice regularly. Devote time to rehearse your speeches, focusing on areas that challenge you the most. Seek feedback from trusted individuals who can provide constructive criticism and help you refine your delivery. Embrace each opportunity as a learning experience, even if you stumble or encounter setbacks. Remember, growth comes from pushing beyond your comfort zone.

By gradually increasing the difficulty level of your speaking engagements, you will not only conquer your fear but also inspire others to face their fears head-on. Your journey will serve as a powerful example, motivating others to embrace their vulnerabilities and unleash their true potential.

In conclusion, conquering fear and empowering yourself to speak with confidence requires a gradual increase in the difficulty level of your speaking engagements. By stepping out of your comfort zone, focusing on niche areas of speech on fear, and regularly practicing, you will develop a strong foundation of confidence and become a source of inspiration for others. Embrace the challenges, learn from each experience, and remember that your voice has the power to make a difference in the lives of many.

Embracing Opportunities for Growth and Learning

In the journey of conquering fear and empowering yourself to speak with confidence, it is essential to recognize the importance of embracing opportunities for growth and learning. Fear can often hold us back from stepping outside of our comfort zones, but it is through these experiences that we truly grow and develop as individuals.

When it comes to delivering a speech on fear, it is crucial to understand that fear itself can be a tremendous source of growth. It is natural to feel anxious or nervous before stepping onto a stage or addressing a crowd, but it is how we choose to face those fears that truly defines our character. By embracing the opportunity to speak on fear, we not only challenge ourselves but also pave the way for personal and professional growth.

One way to embrace these opportunities is by seeking out speaking engagements or workshops that focus specifically on overcoming fear. These platforms provide a safe space to explore your fears and learn techniques to manage them effectively. By actively participating in these activities, you create an environment conducive to growth and learning.

Another powerful way to embrace opportunities for growth and learning is by surrounding yourself with like-minded individuals who share similar fears and aspirations. Joining support groups or engaging in online communities dedicated to public speaking can provide you with a network of individuals who understand and empathize with your struggles. By sharing experiences, exchanging advice, and providing support, you can collectively work towards conquering fear and nurturing personal growth.

It is important to remember that growth and learning are ongoing processes. Even if you stumble or fall along the way, view each setback as an opportunity for learning and improvement. Embrace the lessons learned from these experiences and use them to fuel your determination to overcome fear and speak with confidence.

Ultimately, embracing opportunities for growth and learning is crucial in your journey to conquering fear and speaking with confidence. By actively seeking out these opportunities, surrounding yourself with supportive individuals, and viewing setbacks as opportunities for growth, you will unlock your true potential and become a more empowered and confident speaker.

Remember, everyone has fears and insecurities, but it is those who choose to confront and conquer them that truly stand out. Embrace the opportunities that come your way, push beyond your comfort zone, and watch as your fear transforms into confidence, enabling you to captivate audiences with your words and inspire others to do the same.

In this subchapter, we will explore the crucial process of embracing opportunities for growth and learning when it comes to conquering fear and empowering oneself to speak with confidence. It is a journey that is not only relevant for those specifically focused on overcoming speech-related fears but also for individuals from all walks of life.

Fear is a common emotion that can hinder personal and professional growth. Whether you are delivering a speech on fear or facing any other challenging situation, it is essential to recognize the tremendous potential that lies within these moments. Rather than allowing fear to paralyze us, we can choose to view these opportunities as catalysts for growth and learning.

One of the first steps towards embracing these opportunities is to shift our mindset. Instead of seeing fear as a negative force, we should view it as a sign that we are pushing ourselves outside of our comfort zones. By reframing our perspective, we can start to see fear as a natural part of the learning process, and a necessary step towards personal and professional development.

To truly embrace growth and learning, it is crucial to adopt a growth mindset. This means understanding that our abilities and skills are not fixed, but can be developed through dedication, effort, and a willingness to learn from our failures. By cultivating a growth mindset, we can approach challenges with a sense of curiosity and a belief in our ability to improve over time.

Another powerful tool for embracing growth and learning is seeking opportunities for feedback and reflection. Actively seeking feedback from trusted individuals or mentors can provide valuable insights and help us identify areas for improvement. Additionally, taking the time to reflect on our experiences and learn from both our successes and failures allows us to gain a deeper understanding of ourselves and our abilities.

Finally, embracing opportunities for growth and learning requires a commitment to continuous self-improvement. This involves setting goals, challenging ourselves to step outside of our comfort zones, and seeking out new opportunities for growth. It is through this ongoing process that we can continually refine our skills, increase our confidence, and conquer our fears.

In conclusion, embracing opportunities for growth and learning is a fundamental aspect of conquering fear and empowering oneself to speak with confidence. By shifting our mindset, adopting a growth mindset, seeking feedback and reflection, and committing to continuous self-improvement, we can transform fear into a powerful catalyst for personal and professional growth. Remember, no matter where you are in your journey, every experience provides an opportunity for growth and learning.

Chapter 7: Sustaining Confidence and Overcoming Setbacks

Maintaining a Positive Mindset

In the journey of conquering fear and empowering ourselves to speak with confidence, one of the most vital aspects is maintaining a positive mindset. Our mindset plays a significant role in shaping our thoughts, actions, and ultimately, our ability to overcome fear and deliver powerful speeches on this topic. Whether you are a public speaker, student, or simply someone seeking personal growth, cultivating a positive mindset is crucial for success.

First and foremost, it is important to recognize that fear is a natural emotion that everyone experiences. However, it is our response to fear that determines whether it will hinder or enhance our abilities. By maintaining a positive mindset, we can reframe our perception of fear as a catalyst for growth and development rather than a barrier. Embracing this perspective allows us to approach public speaking on fear with enthusiasm, curiosity, and a willingness to learn.

One effective strategy to maintain a positive mindset is through the power of affirmations. Affirmations are positive statements that reinforce our belief in our abilities. By repeating affirmations such as "I am confident and capable of overcoming fear," we reprogram our subconscious mind to focus on our strengths rather than our weaknesses. This shift in mindset empowers us to approach speeches on fear with self-assurance and conviction.

Another important aspect of maintaining a positive mindset is surrounding ourselves with a supportive network. Seek out individuals who inspire and uplift you, whether it be mentors, friends, or fellow speakers. Sharing experiences, seeking advice, and receiving encouragement from like-minded individuals can significantly boost your morale and solidify your belief in your own abilities.

Additionally, practicing gratitude can have a profound impact on our mindset. Taking the time to acknowledge and appreciate the progress we have made, no matter how small, reinforces a positive outlook. Gratitude shifts our focus from what we lack to what we have accomplished, fostering a sense of confidence and motivation to continue growing.

Lastly, it is essential to embrace failure as a stepping stone to success. Fear of failure often hinders our progress and dampens our mindset. However, by reframing failure as an opportunity for growth and learning, we can adopt a positive mindset even in the face of setbacks. Each experience, whether successful or not, brings valuable lessons that contribute to our personal and professional development.

In conclusion, maintaining a positive mindset is vital in conquering fear and empowering ourselves to speak with confidence on the topic. By shifting our perspective, practicing affirmations, surrounding ourselves with a supportive network, expressing gratitude, and embracing failure, we can cultivate a mindset that propels us forward on our journey of personal growth and fearlessness. Remember, with the right mindset, you have the power to overcome any fear and deliver impactful speeches with confidence.

In the journey of conquering fear and empowering yourself to speak with confidence, maintaining a positive mindset plays a crucial role. Your mindset can either be your greatest ally or your biggest obstacle when it comes to overcoming the fear of public speaking. It is essential to cultivate a positive outlook as you navigate the challenges of delivering a speech on fear.

The power of positive thinking cannot be underestimated. When you approach speaking engagements with a positive mindset, you are better equipped to handle any obstacles that may arise. Positivity fuels your determination and resilience, allowing you to face your fears head-on. By maintaining a positive mindset, you can transform any negative thoughts or self-doubt into motivation and self-belief.

One effective way to maintain a positive mindset is through affirmations. Affirmations are positive statements that you repeat to yourself regularly, such as "I am confident and capable of delivering a powerful speech" or "I embrace challenges and grow from them." By consistently affirming positive beliefs, you reprogram your subconscious mind, replacing self-limiting beliefs with empowering thoughts.

Another valuable tool to maintain a positive mindset is visualization. Visualize yourself standing confidently on stage, delivering your speech with passion and conviction. Picture the audience engaged and inspired by your words. By vividly imagining success, your subconscious mind becomes familiar with the experience, making it easier for you to manifest it in reality.

Surrounding yourself with positive influences is also essential. Seek out individuals who uplift and support you in your journey. Join public speaking groups or communities where you can share your experiences, learn from others, and receive constructive feedback. Engaging with like-minded individuals who understand your fears and aspirations can help you stay motivated and maintain a positive mindset.

Additionally, practicing gratitude can significantly contribute to a positive mindset. Take a moment each day to reflect on the things you are grateful for, whether it be the opportunity to speak, supportive friends and family, or personal growth. Gratitude shifts your focus from fear and anxiety to appreciation and positivity, allowing you to approach speaking engagements with a grateful heart.

In conclusion, maintaining a positive mindset is paramount in conquering fear and empowering yourself to speak with confidence. By incorporating affirmations, visualization, surrounding yourself with positive influences, and practicing gratitude, you can cultivate a mindset that supports your growth as a speaker. Embrace the power of positivity and watch as you transform your fear into fuel for success. Remember, you have the potential to deliver impactful speeches and inspire others – all it takes is a positive mindset.

Cultivating a Supportive Network

In the journey to conquer fear and empower yourself to speak with confidence, cultivating a supportive network is an essential step. Surrounding yourself with individuals who understand and empathize with your struggles can make a significant difference in your ability to overcome fear and deliver powerful speeches.

Everyone, regardless of their background or experience, can benefit from building a strong support system. Whether you are new to public speaking or have been battling fear for years, having a network of like-minded individuals can provide the encouragement and motivation needed to push through any obstacles.

A supportive network can take various forms. It may consist of friends, family, colleagues, or fellow speech enthusiasts who share your passion for conquering fear. These individuals can offer a listening ear, provide constructive feedback, and share their own experiences and tips for success. Through their support, you will gain insights and strategies to overcome fear, allowing you to speak with confidence.

Furthermore, a supportive network can help you practice and refine your speeches. Organizing regular mock presentations or participating in speaking clubs with your network allows for a safe and nurturing environment to hone your skills. Constructive criticism from trusted individuals will help you identify areas for improvement, build your confidence, and refine your delivery.

Additionally, a supportive network can offer emotional support during challenging times. Fear can be overwhelming, and having someone who understands your struggles and can provide encouragement can be immensely helpful. Your network can share stories of their own triumphs over fear, reminding you that you are not alone in this journey.

In cultivating a supportive network, it is important to be proactive. Seek out individuals who share your interest in conquering fear and speaking with confidence. Attend workshops, seminars, or join online communities where you can connect with like-minded individuals. Engage in conversations, share your experiences, and be open to learning from others.

Remember, building a supportive network takes time and effort, but the benefits are immeasurable. By surrounding yourself with individuals who understand your fears and aspirations, you will gain the support, motivation, and guidance needed to conquer fear and deliver impactful speeches. Together, you can empower each other to overcome any obstacles and confidently share your message with the world.

In the journey of conquering fear and empowering yourself to speak with confidence, one of the most crucial elements is cultivating a supportive network. Regardless of your background or the niche you belong to, having a strong support system can make a world of difference in overcoming the fear of public speaking. This subchapter will explore the importance of building a network and provide practical tips on how to do so effectively.

First and foremost, it's essential to recognize that fear of speaking is a common experience shared by many. You are not alone in this struggle, and by surrounding yourself with like-minded individuals, you can find solace, encouragement, and inspiration. Seek out communities, both online and offline, that focus on speech on fear. Attend workshops, join public speaking clubs, or participate in group activities that promote personal growth and development. Engaging with individuals who understand and empathize with your journey will provide the support you need to navigate through your fears.

Additionally, it is crucial to identify mentors or role models who have successfully overcome their fear of public speaking. Learning from those who have conquered the same challenges can provide valuable insights and guidance. Reach out to individuals who have excelled in public speaking and ask for advice or mentorship. Their expertise and experience can serve as a beacon of hope and motivation, showing you that it is possible to overcome your fear and speak confidently.

Building a supportive network also entails surrounding yourself with friends and family who believe in your abilities. Share your goals and aspirations with them, and let them know how important it is to you to conquer your fear of speaking. Their encouragement, love, and support will boost your confidence and provide a safety net during challenging times.

Remember, cultivating a supportive network is a two-way street. Be willing to offer support and encouragement to others who are on a similar journey. By uplifting and inspiring others, you create a positive and nurturing environment that fosters personal growth and empowerment. Share your knowledge, experiences, and resources with others, and you will find that the support you receive will multiply.

In conclusion, cultivating a supportive network is instrumental in conquering fear and empowering yourself to speak with confidence. Surrounding yourself with like-minded individuals, seeking mentors or role models, and leaning on the support of friends and family will provide you with the strength and encouragement needed to overcome your fear of public speaking. Additionally, by offering support to others, you contribute to a positive and nurturing environment that fosters growth and empowerment for everyone. Remember, you are not alone in this journey, and with the right network, you can conquer your fear and speak with confidence.

Learning from Failures and Bouncing Back Stronger

Failure is an inevitable part of life. It is through failure that we learn, grow, and ultimately become stronger individuals. In the journey of conquering fear and empowering ourselves to speak with confidence, it is essential to embrace failures as stepping stones towards success. This subchapter aims to shed light on the importance of learning from failures and how they can help us bounce back stronger.

When it comes to delivering speeches on fear, it is natural to feel anxious and apprehensive. Fear of public speaking is one of the most common fears people face. However, instead of allowing failures to discourage us, we should view them as valuable learning experiences. Each failure provides us with an opportunity to reflect on our weaknesses and areas for improvement. By analyzing what went wrong, we can identify the necessary steps to enhance our public speaking skills.

Learning from failures involves embracing a growth mindset. Rather than viewing setbacks as permanent, we should see them as temporary obstacles that can be overcome. By adopting this mindset, we can develop resilience and the ability to bounce back stronger. It is essential to remember that even the most successful speakers have experienced failures along their journey. They learned from their mistakes, refined their techniques, and eventually mastered the art of confident public speaking.

Furthermore, failures provide valuable insights into our own fears and insecurities. By acknowledging and understanding these fears, we can work towards overcoming them. It is crucial to recognize that failure is not a reflection of our worth or abilities; instead, it is a stepping stone towards personal growth. Embracing failure as a part of the learning process allows us to build confidence and resilience in the face of adversity.

In conclusion, learning from failures and bouncing back stronger is an integral part of conquering fear and empowering ourselves to speak with confidence. By embracing failures as learning experiences, adopting a growth mindset, and understanding our fears, we can transform setbacks into opportunities for growth. Remember, failure is not the end but a crucial step towards success. Embrace failures, learn from them, and use them as fuel to propel yourself towards becoming a confident and powerful speaker.

Chapter 8: Embracing Fear as a Catalyst for Personal Growth

Shifting Perspective on Fear

In this subchapter, we delve into the fascinating and transformative concept of shifting our perspective on fear. Fear is a universal human emotion that has the power to paralyze us and hold us back from reaching our true potential. However, by understanding fear and learning to view it from a different angle, we can harness its energy and use it to our advantage.

Fear is often associated with negative connotations and seen as something to be avoided at all costs. We are taught from a young age to steer clear of fear, and our natural instinct is to run away from it. But what if we could change our relationship with fear? What if we could see fear as a valuable tool rather than a hindrance?

When it comes to public speaking, fear can be a significant barrier. Many of us dread standing in front of a crowd and delivering a speech. We are afraid of being judged, of making mistakes, and of being exposed. However, by shifting our perspective on fear, we can transform this anxiety into a powerful ally.

Imagine viewing fear as a sign that you are stepping out of your comfort zone, pushing your boundaries, and growing as an individual. Instead of avoiding fear, embrace it as a signal that you are on the right path towards personal and professional growth. This shift in perspective allows you to reframe fear as a positive force, motivating you to take risks and challenge yourself.

By understanding that fear is a natural response to the unknown, you can learn to manage it effectively. Acknowledge your fear, but don't let it control you. Practice deep breathing techniques, positive self-talk, and visualization exercises to calm your nerves and boost your confidence. Remember, fear is not an indication of weakness, but rather a testament to your courage and bravery.

In this subchapter, we will explore various strategies and techniques to help you shift your perspective on fear. Through personal anecdotes, expert insights, and practical exercises, you will gain the tools necessary to conquer your fear and speak with confidence.

Whether you are a seasoned speaker or someone who wants to overcome their fear of public speaking, this subchapter is designed to empower you. By embracing fear and shifting your perspective, you can unlock your true potential and become a powerful and persuasive communicator.

Join us on this journey of self-discovery and learn to conquer your fear, empowering yourself to speak with confidence. Together, let's change our relationship with fear and embrace it as a catalyst for personal and professional growth.

Harnessing Fear to Fuel Motivation and Achievement

Fear is a powerful emotion that often holds us back from reaching our full potential. It can paralyze us, making it difficult to take risks and pursue our dreams. However, what if we could turn fear into a driving force for motivation and achievement? In this subchapter, we will explore how to harness fear and use it as a catalyst for personal growth and success, particularly in the context of delivering speeches on fear.

Fear is a natural response to the unknown or unfamiliar. It is our body's way of protecting us from potential danger. However, fear can also be a sign that we are stepping outside of our comfort zone and challenging ourselves. By reframing our perception of fear, we can transform it from a hindrance into a valuable tool for growth.

One way to harness fear is to acknowledge and embrace it. Instead of trying to suppress or ignore our fears, we can use them as a source of motivation. By acknowledging our fears, we can identify the underlying reasons for them and work towards addressing them. This self-awareness allows us to better understand ourselves and our motivations, paving the way for personal growth.

Another technique is to visualize success. When delivering a speech on fear, imagine yourself delivering it with confidence and receiving a positive response from the audience. Visualizing success helps to rewire our brain, making it more likely that we will achieve our goals. This technique also helps to reduce anxiety and instill a sense of self-belief.

Additionally, setting achievable goals can help us overcome fear and fuel motivation. Break down the task of delivering a speech on fear into smaller, manageable steps. By accomplishing these smaller goals, we build confidence and momentum towards our ultimate objective. This gradual approach allows us to confront our fears in a controlled and manageable way.

Lastly, seeking support from others can provide the encouragement and reassurance needed to overcome fear. Surround yourself with a supportive network of friends, family, or mentors who believe in your abilities. Their encouragement and feedback can boost your confidence and help you navigate any challenges that may arise.

Harnessing fear to fuel motivation and achievement is a powerful approach that can transform our lives. By reframing our perception of fear, visualizing success, setting achievable goals, and seeking support, we can overcome our fears and accomplish great things. Whether it is delivering a speech on fear or pursuing any other goal, harnessing fear can empower us to speak with confidence and achieve our dreams.

Empowering Yourself to Speak with Confidence

Speaking in public can be a daunting task for many individuals, as the fear of being judged, making mistakes, or forgetting important points often hinders their ability to communicate effectively. However, with the right tools and mindset, anyone can conquer their fear and empower themselves to speak with confidence. In this subchapter, we will explore various techniques and strategies that will help you overcome your fear of public speaking and deliver impactful speeches on the topic of fear.

Firstly, it is crucial to acknowledge that fear is a natural human response. It is not something to be ashamed of, but rather an opportunity for growth. By reframing your perspective on fear, you can transform it into a catalyst for personal development. Embrace the discomfort and view it as a sign that you are pushing yourself beyond your comfort zone.

Next, preparation is key to building confidence in public speaking. Spend ample time researching and organizing your speech on fear. Understand your target audience and tailor your message accordingly. Practice your speech multiple times, paying attention to your body language, tone of voice, and pacing. Rehearsing will not only familiarize you with the material but also boost your confidence and reduce anxiety.

Moreover, it is important to remember that authenticity is paramount when delivering a speech on fear. Speak from the heart and share personal experiences or anecdotes that resonate with the audience. Being genuine and vulnerable will establish a connection and engage your listeners on a deeper level. Remember, everyone experiences fear, and by sharing your own struggles, you can inspire others to confront their own fears.

Additionally, mastering the art of storytelling can greatly enhance your ability to captivate an audience. Craft compelling narratives that illustrate the impact of fear in different contexts. Use vivid language, imagery, and emotions to create a powerful narrative arc that leaves a lasting impression. A well-told story can evoke empathy, inspire action, and ignite change.

Lastly, seek opportunities to practice and refine your public speaking skills. Join local clubs or organizations that offer platforms for public speaking. Embrace constructive feedback and continuously work on improving your delivery. The more you expose yourself to speaking in front of others, the more comfortable and confident you will become.

In conclusion, conquering the fear of public speaking and empowering yourself to speak with confidence is a journey that requires time, effort, and perseverance. By reframing your perspective on fear, preparing meticulously, being authentic, using storytelling techniques, and seeking opportunities for practice, you can overcome your fears and deliver impactful speeches on the topic of fear. Remember, your voice matters, and by sharing your insights and experiences, you have the power to inspire and empower others to confront their own fears.

Conclusion: Your Journey to Fearless Communication Begins Now!

Congratulations! You have reached the end of this empowering book, "Conquering Fear: Empowering Yourself to Speak with Confidence." Throughout this journey, we have explored the depths of fear and its impact on our ability to communicate effectively. Now, it is time for you to take what you have learned and embark on your own journey towards fearless communication.

Fear is a natural response that we all experience when faced with the unknown or stepping out of our comfort zones. However, it should not hinder us from expressing ourselves and sharing our thoughts and ideas with the world. By conquering fear, we can unlock our true potential and become confident communicators.

In this book, we have delved into various techniques and strategies to help you overcome your fear of speaking. We have explored the power of positive self-talk, visualization, and deep breathing exercises. We have also discussed the importance of preparation and practice in building confidence and reducing anxiety.

Now it is time for you to put these tools into action. Embrace your fear and face it head-on. Remember that you are not alone in this journey. Countless individuals have overcome their fear of public speaking, and so can you.

To begin your journey, start by setting small, achievable goals. Perhaps it is giving a presentation to a small group of friends or volunteering to speak at a local community event. Celebrate each step you take towards overcoming your fear, no matter how small it may seem.

Always remember that progress takes time and effort. There may be setbacks along the way, but do not let them discourage you. Use these setbacks as learning opportunities and keep pushing forward. Surround yourself with a supportive network of friends, family, or even a public speaking coach who can offer guidance and encouragement.

The journey to fearless communication is not only about conquering your fear but also about embracing your unique voice and perspective. Your thoughts and ideas have value, and the world deserves to hear them. By overcoming your fear, you can become a powerful and influential speaker, capable of inspiring and impacting others.

So, take the first step today. Start your journey towards fearless communication. Believe in yourself, embrace your fears, and watch as you blossom into a confident and compelling speaker. The world is waiting to hear your voice.

Milton Keynes UK
Ingram Content Group UK Ltd.
UKHW020623291123
433416UK00016B/1123